Gifford Pinchot, Edward A Bowers

1. Government forestry abroad

Gifford Pinchot, Edward A Bowers

1. Government forestry abroad

ISBN/EAN: 9783337141646

Printed in Europe, USA, Canada, Australia, Japan

Cover: Foto ©Suzi / pixelio.de

More available books at **www.hansebooks.com**

PUBLICATIONS

OF THE

AMERICAN ECONOMIC ASSOCIATION.

Vol. VI. No. 3.   Six numbers a year
Price $4.00 a year.

I.
Government Forestry Abroad,
By GIFFORD PINCHOT.

II.
The Present Condition of the Forests on the Public Lands,
By EDWARD A. BOWERS,
Secretary of the American Forestry Association.
(Formerly Inspector of Public Lands.)

III.
Practicability of an American Forest Administration,
By B. E. FERNOW,
Chief of Forestry Division, Department of Agriculture, Washington, D. C.

AMERICAN ECONOMIC ASSOCIATION.

May, 1891.

COPYRIGHT, 1891, BY AMERICAN ECONOMIC ASSOCIATION.

BALTIMORE:
FROM THE PRESS OF GUGGENHEIMER, WEIL & CO.
1891.

TABLE OF CONTENTS.

	PAGE
I. GOVERNMENT FORESTRY ABROAD. By GIFFORD PINCHOT	5
Germany	9
France	24
Switzerland	32
Australia	42
India	45
South Africa	50
Other Countries	52
II. THE PRESENT CONDITION OF THE FOREST ON THE PUBLIC LANDS. By EDWARD A. BOWERS	55
III. PRACTICABILITY OF AN AMERICAN FOREST ADMINISTRATION. By B. E. FERNOW	75
IV. APPENDIX: PROPOSED BILL	93

The three papers on Forest Administration here printed together were read at the joint session of the American Economic Association and the American Forestry Association, at Washington, D. C., December 30, 1890.

Government Forestry Abroad.

BY

GIFFORD PINCHOT.

Government Forestry Abroad.

BY GIFFORD PINCHOT.

The following article has been rather hastily prepared from such materials and experience as the writer was able to command, and while from the nature of the case it cannot claim to be a comprehensive treatment of the subject, it is believed that the statements and statistics which it contains are accurate.

Germany, France and Switzerland have been dwelt upon more at length, both because forestry has reached a wider development there, and because the writer can speak concerning them from personal observation.

The history of the forest has developed itself along similar lines in all the countries of Europe. Its course in the central part of the Continent, which may be taken as fairly representative of what it was elsewhere, is thus briefly summarized.

At first the forest held the same relation to man as to the game upon which he lived. His demand upon it was insignificant, but, as he advanced in the scale of civilization, he began to call upon the forest for greater supplies of timber, and especially for the pasturage of his herds. Until comparatively recent times this was the chief service which gave the wood

lands value. The increasing density of population
and the more complicated needs of life then gave
gradual rise to more vigorous attacks upon the forest.
For a time the demand was small and the areas cut
over easily covered themselves with young growth.
The forest renewed itself and maintained its productive power. But, as the demand increased, the
areas cut over increased with it, and the actual regrowth no longer kept pace with the quantity of
timber which it was called upon to yield. At the
same time the land needed for agriculture was being
taken from the timbered area, and the wood lands,
attacked along two lines, were beginning to suffer
seriously.

"It is true," says Dr. Gayer,[1] "that the forest belonged at that time chiefly to the herdsmen and the game, but the steadily increasing tendency to destruction of a growing population made the general cultivation of the chase an undoubted advantage to the forest. Indeed the hunter has been at all times one of its best friends. For numerous acts of violence may be referred to, extending over the whole of mediæval times, as a result of which much free land belonging to the early communities, or the rights to its enjoyment, passed in course of time into the hands of the rulers. From a legal standpoint these are indeed events to be deplored, and from them the oppressive burden of actual prescriptive rights takes its rise, but the present extensive State forest holdings in Germany have chiefly to thank this universal love of venerie for their existence.

. . . .

"It is unquestionably true that the forests have been at no time in a more deplorable condition than in the second half of the Middle Ages, and thence on to the middle of the last century. The results which must follow this condition of affairs were evident, and led to the most serious fears of a widespread timber famine. And although this foreboding, as it filled the minds of men toward the end of the Mediæval period, and as it was brought to the attention of the people through numerous publications, may have been exaggerated, nevertheless, in view of the commercial relations of the

---

[1] Der Wald im Wechsel der Zeiten. Inaugural address as Rector of the University of Munich, November, 1889.

time and the narrow boundaries of supply, it was on the whole by no means unjustified. It gave, at least, the first impulse to economy. Under the influence of this universal sentiment, but perhaps caused even more by the interest in hunting and in the security of the rights of property, a gradual change for the better appeared in the destiny of the forest. Its importance as a national treasure had at all events penetrated the minds of the more intelligent classes.

. . . .

"There begins now a time of restless work in the forest, a time of struggle for its preservation and rehabilitation, the results of which no other nation has realized so fully as the German.

"Apart from the measures which were demanded by the security of property and the economical ordering of forest utilization, the efforts of the forester were chiefly directed to the regeneration of the forest. This was accomplished in those regions which had partially escaped destruction by the assistance of the free regenerative power of nature, in the totally devastated areas by artificial means. The rational treatment of the wood lands had begun."

All forest management may be said to rest on two closely related facts which are so self-evident that they might almost be called axioms of forestry, but which, like other axioms, lead to conclusions of far-reaching application. These are, first, that trees require many years to reach merchantable size; and, secondly, that a forest crop cannot be taken every year from the same land. From the last statement it follows that a definite, far-seeing plan is necessary for the rational management of any forest, from the first: that forest property is safest under the supervision of some imperishable guardian; or, in other words, of the State.

GERMANY.

It is natural in treating the subject of State forestry to begin with Germany, since it is here that it has reached its furthest development and most stable condition. In Germany, then, the forests cover an area of 13,908,398 hectares, or 26 per cent. of the total surface of the country. It is extremely significant, in view of the popular talk about the "inexhaustible" forest resources of the United States, to note that the latest available data put the percentage of wooded land in our country also at 26 per cent. It is true that the relative density of population in the two countries is a factor which enters largely into such a comparison, but it is equally true as regards the relative economy in the use of wood, and the fact that Germany is very far from supplying her own demand for timber. Further, the contrast between the permanent productive powers of the German and American wood lands, as they stand at present, adds another somber tint to the picture of our condition. In Germany, the State either owns or controls about two-thirds of the forest area, and for these lands the point of lowest production has been past. It is coming for us at a time when the need of timber is at its highest.

It is necessary when dealing with forest policy in the German Empire to treat independently the different States of which it is composed. Differences in forest organization and management have arisen through differences in politics and geography, even a superficial examination of which would exceed both the space and the scope of the present paper, and it is fortunately the less needful to go into so extended a discussion, because one common principle lies at the root of forest policy in each of them, and may be fully illustrated by reference to any one. This principle, special to no country or form of government, holds that "the State is the guardian of all public interests." It is in its interpretation that, for the purposes of this paper, its chief interest lies. From this point of view "public interests" must be taken to mean all interests other than private ones. So understood, this maxim may be said to sum up the forest policy of nearly all the nations of Europe, as well under republican as under governments of a distinctly paternal character.

The Kingdom of Prussia, both as the head of the German Bund and as the State which has developed the forest organization most worthy to be taken as an example, will furnish the completest illustration.

Covering an area of some 8,153,946 hectares, the forests of Prussia occupy 23.4 per cent. of the total surface of the country. Of this wood land it may be said roughly that one-third is stocked with deciduous trees, and two-thirds with the less demanding conifers, a reversal of the old conditions, which is largely due to the deterioration of the soil and to the fact that the richer ground has been rightly claimed for agricultural uses. The ownership, a point of capital importance in relation to our subject, is divided as follows: To the State belong nearly 2,718,-256 hectares, or 29 per cent.; to towns, village communities and other public bodies, 1,302,508 hectares, or 16 per cent., and to private owners 4,382,251 hectares, or 55 per cent.

The relation of the State to the forests which it owns is simple and rational, based as it is on the idea that its ownership will be permanent.

Holding it as a duty to preserve the wood lands for the present share which they take in the economy of the nation, the State has recognized as well the obligation to hand down its forest wealth unimpaired to future generations. It has recognized and respected equally the place which the forest holds in relation to agriculture and in the economy of nature, and hence feels itself doubly bound to protect its wood lands.

In a word, it has seen that in its direct and indirect influence, the forest plays a most important part in the story of human progress, and that the advance of civilization only serves to make it more indispensable. It has, therefore, steadily refused to deliver its forests to more or less speedy destruction, by allowing them to pass into the hands of shorter lived and less provident owners. Even in the times of greatest financial difficulty, when Prussia was overrun and nearly annihilated by the French, the idea of selling the State forests was never seriously entertained.

But the government of Prussia has not stopped here. Protection standing alone is irrational and incomplete. The cases where a forest reaches its highest usefulness by simply existing are rare. The immense capital which the State wood lands represent is not permitted to lie idle, and the forest, as a timber producer, has taken its place among the permanent features of the land. The government has done the only wise thing by managing its own forests through its own forest officers.

The organization of the Forest Service is briefly as follows: At its head stands the Department, or more correctly, the Ministry of Agriculture. State lands and forests, which exercises general supervision over forest affairs through the medium of the (Oberlandforstmeister) chief of Forest Service. A part of this central office is the Bureau of Forest Surveys and Working Plans, a factor of very great importance in the general organization. A working plan is the scheme according to which the technical business of a forest range is carried out. "Its object," says Dr. Judeich,[1] "is so to order the management of a forest in time and space as to fulfill to the utmost the objects of this management." The following subdivision of the general subject of working plans is taken from his admirable work, "Die Forsteinrichtung." The first section is entitled "Preliminary Work," under which are included: forest surveys, forest or timber estimating (which includes "the investigation of all conditions inherent in the forest which have an influence on its present yield, or which are of importance for the calculation of its yield in the future;" that is, the very thorough study and description of both soil and timber), a study of the general and external conditions by which it is affected (its topography, history, ownership, nature of the surrounding land and people, and any other considerations which may influence its management), and, lastly, maps and records.

The second section, which may be called Forest Division for want of a better English name, considers the formation of ranges, each of which is in charge of an executive officer, then the division of the range into units of management called blocks, each of which is treated to a certain extent independently of the others, and into compartments, which are generally well over a hundred acres in extent, and are marked on the ground by open lanes and boundary stones. This second section contains also less important matters which cannot be touched on here.

---
[1] *Die Forsteinrichtung.* 4th Ed. Dresden, 1885.

The third section, Determination of the Yield, explains the various methods of calculating and fixing the amount of timber which a given forest may be safely called upon to yield.

The next section treats of the construction of the working plans proper; that is, "of that document in which the essential results of the preliminary work, the determination of the yield and the regulation of the management are so put together that they may serve as a guide . to the executive officer of the range."

The final section relates to the posting and continuation of the working plans, especially as regards the periodic revisions, which take place in general at intervals of five and ten years.

Next in authority to the department just mentioned is the Bezirksregierung, a council in charge of one of the thirty-five minor divisions of the Prussian State, which has full control over forest business within its sphere of action. The members of the controlling staff, the Oberförstmeister and Forstmeister, are also members of this council. Their duties lie in the inspection of the officers of the executive staff, of whom there are 681 in Prussia. These officers, styled Oberförster, are charged with the actual management of the public forest lands, and it is on them that the security of public interest in the forests chiefly rests. Upon their selection and education the utmost care and forethought are expended.

Their course of training, one which has produced perhaps the most efficient forest staff of the present day, is briefly as follows: It begins, after graduation from a gymnasium, with a year of practical work under some experienced Oberförster, to enter which the candidate is required to show, besides his certificate of graduation, that he is under twenty-two years of age; that he has certain moral and physical qualities, and that his financial resources are sufficient to carry him through his whole forest education. The object of this preparatory year is to introduce the beginner to the forest and its management; to enable him to become acquainted with the more important forest trees; to take part in planting and felling and the protection of the forest; to do a little surveying, and last, but by no means least, to learn to hunt. It may be said in passing that the love of hunting, which the Prussian forest service is careful to encourage, has very much to do with the faithfulness and efficiency of its individual members. Great stress is rightly laid on this year of preparatory work, chiefly because of the vastly greater force and reality which it gives to the subsequent theoretical teaching. As one who has suffered from the lack of it, I may perhaps be permitted to bear my testimony to the value of a custom which is unfortunately less widely extended than its merits deserve; but which I hope to see one day established in the forest schools of our land.

The young Prussian forester who has had the good fortune to pass through this preliminary year next spends two years at a forest school, presumably either Münden or Neustadt Eberswalde, both of which are in Prussia, and like all other similar German schools, are supported by the State. The candidate may, if he chooses, attend any of the other forest schools, of which Germany numbers six (Aschaffenburg and the Forest School of the Munich University, which together form one complete institution: Tharand, Tübingen, Karlsruhe, Giesen and Eisenach), but he must cover the same ground as at the institutions which are standard. The technical school is followed by a year of jurisprudence and political economy at some university, and the young forester then comes up for the first State examination. He must present with his credentials the maps and field notes of a plot surveyed and a level run, as well as a timber map covering at least 1.235 acres, all his own work. The examination itself bears first on forestry, in which it requires a thorough knowledge of the general theory as to silviculture, working plans, calculation of the volume and yield of standing timber, its capital and selling value, the utilization of forest produce, forest technology, protection and police, and forest history and literature. In mathematics it demands about what is included up to the second year of one of our colleges, and in surveying the requirements are somewhat larger. Zoology, botany and mineralogy, especially the second, are strongly insisted on, while chemistry, physics and law command a smaller share of attention.

The examination is followed by at least two years of travel and work, during which the candidate, now promoted to the title of referendar, must perfect himself in the field and office management of a forest range. For this purpose he is required to spend five months in the practical administration of a range, under the responsibility of an Oberförster, and four months in the preparation of working plans. Half a year, including the months from December to May, is to be passed in the discharge of all the duties of an ordinary forest guard. During this time the referendar is personally responsible for all that goes on in his beat, which must be the same for the whole period. At the end of this rather lengthy preparation comes the much-dreaded final examination, which, like the first, is held partly in doors and partly in the forest. This second test dwells more especially, apart from forestry proper, on law, political economy, finance, forest policy, and the organization of the forest service, but without slighting the laws and lore of hunting.

The referendar now becomes forest assessor, and is at length eligible for serious paid employment. The actual career of the forester can hardly be said to begin, however, until the appointment as Oberförster, for which the assessor has no sort of guarantee, and which may delay its coming for from six to twelve years. That once obtained, the list of promotion lies open, and includes every grade up to the highest. Still, it must be said that, as a rule, the Prussian Oberförster is wholly satisfied with his position, and very often unwilling to exchange it for one of greater honor and profit.

That it should be so is scarcely to be wondered at. The Oberförster, with almost independent control of a range of some 10,000 acres, and, what is of first importance to him, with an exclusive right to the excellent shooting which it usually offers, lives a healthy, active life, about equally divided between the woods, his office and his friends. His pay, which may reach 6,400 marks, including a consolidated allowance for horses and the incidentals of his office work, is ridiculously low from our standpoint, but entirely sufficient from his. Promotion means a change from the moderate activity of overseeing the planting and felling of his forest, and the quiet of home life, to the constant activity of travel. The stimulus which ambition fails to give is supplied by the admirable *esprit de corps* which pervades the whole body of forest officers, and forms here, as elsewhere, the best security for the efficiency and healthy tone of the service.

Immediately subordinate to the members of the executive staff are the various grades of forest guards, upon whom the protection of the forest directly and exclusively rests. In general, each guard is in charge of one of the five beats into which the average range is divided. "The forester (I quote from the Service Instructions) must protect the beat entrusted to him against unlawful utilization, theft and injury, and see to it that the forest and game laws are observed. He is charged with the execution of the felling, planting and other forest work under the orders of the Oberförster, and he alone delivers all forest produce, on receipt of written instructions, to the persons qualified to receive it."

The training of the protective staff is provided for with a care which in any other land might be thought more suitable for officers of a higher grade, and a period of preparation only less long than that for Oberförster stands before the beginner.

But lest the necessity for so long a course of preparatory work should seem unduly to enhance the difficulties of forest management, it should be noted here that in countries whose grade of excellence in forest matters is closely second to that of Germany the schooling of forest officers is very considerably shorter. There will be occasion to refer to this matter further on.

Such is in outline the organization of the Prussian forest service. The principles upon which it rests are thus stated by Donner, now Oberlandforstmeister. in a work which carries all the weight of an official document.[1] He says:

"The fundamental rules for the management of State forests are these: First, to keep rigidly within the bounds of conservative treatment; and secondly, to attain, consistently with such treatment, the greatest output of most useful products in the shortest time."

And again:

"The State believes itself bound, in the administration of its forests, to keep in view the common good of the people, and that as well with respect to the lasting satisfaction of the demand for timber and other forest produce, as to the numerous other purposes which the forest serves. It holds fast the duty to treat the Government wood lands as a trust held for the nation as a whole, to the end that it may enjoy for the present the highest satisfaction of its needs for forest produce and the protection which the forest gives, and for all future time, at least an equal share of equal blessings."

The same authority elsewhere formulates the general status of the forest, as follows:

"The forest is a trust handed down from former times, whose value lies not only in its immediate production of wood, but also essentially in the benefit to agriculture of its immediate influence on climate, weather protection in various ways, the conservation of the soil, etc. The forest has significance not only for the present nor for its owner alone; it has significance as well for the future and for the whole of the people."

With respect to the second class of forest property, that belonging to towns, villages and other public bodies, it is again impossible to speak for the whole of Germany except upon the broadest lines. The State everywhere exercises oversight and a degree of control over the management of these forests, but the sphere of its action varies within very wide limits. Even within the individual states it does not remain

---
[1] *Die Forstliche Verhältnisse Preussens*, 2d ed., Berlin, 1883.

the same. Thus far, however, the action of the Government is alike not only throughout Prussia but in all parts of Germany. It prevents absolutely the treatment of any forest of this class under improvident or wasteful methods; nor does it allow any measure to be carried into effect which may deprive posterity of the enjoyment which it has a right to expect. How far the details vary may be gathered from the fact that while in the Prussian provinces of Rhineland and Westphalia the village communities appoint their own forest officers and manage their own forests, subject only to a tolerably close oversight on the part of the controlling staff, in the former Duchy of Nassau, now Prussian territory, their share in the management does not extend beyond the right to sell the timber cut under the direction of the Government Oberförster, the right and obligation to pay for all the planting and other improvements which may be deemed necessary, and the rather hollow privilege of expressing their opinion. But however galling so extensive an interference with the rights of property may appear, it is none the less unquestionably true that in France, as well as in Germany, the State management of communal forests lies at the root of the prosperity of a very large proportion of the peasant population, and the evils which have attended its withdrawal in individual cases are notorious. While on the one hand villages whose taxes are wholly paid by their forests are by no means rare, on the other the sale of communal forest property in certain parts of Germany in 1848 has been followed with deplorable regularity by the impoverishment of the villages which were unwise enough to allow it.

The relations of the State to the third class of forests, those belonging to private proprietors, are of a much less intimate nature. The basis of these relations is, however, the same. To quote again from Donner, "The duty of the State to sustain and further the well being of its citizens regarded as an imperishable whole, implies for the Government the right and the duty to subject the management of all forests to its inspection and control." This intervention is to be carried, however, "only so far as may be necessary to obviate the dangers which an unrestrained utilization of the forest by its owners threatens to excite, and the rights of property are to be respected to the utmost consistently with such a result." Prussia, of all the German countries, has respected these rights most highly, and the Government exerts practically no restraining influence except where the evident results of deforestation would be seriously dangerous. Here it may and does guard most jealously the wood lands, whose presence is a necessary safeguard against certain of the more destructive phenomena of nature, and which have been called in general protection forests. Of their many sided influence so much has been said and written of late in America—both truly and falsely—that no farther reference to the subject seems needful.

The State leaves open a way of escape for the private proprietor who finds himself unwilling to suffer such restriction of his rights for the public good, and shows itself willing to buy up areas not only of protection forest but also of less vitally important wood lands. On the other hand, it is ready, with a broadness of view which the zeal of forest authorities sometimes unfortunately excludes, to give up to pri-

vate ownership lands which, by reason of their soil
and situation, will contribute better to the common-
wealth under cultivation than as forest. In this way
the forests whose preservation is most important are
gradually passing into the hands of the State; yet
the total area of its wood lands is increasing but
slowly.

The policy of State aid in the afforestation of waste
lands important through their situation on high
ground or otherwise is fully recognized (a notable
example exists upon the Hohe Venn near Aix-la-
Chapelle), but the absence of considerable mountain
chains has given to this branch of Government influence very much less prominence than in the Alps of
Austria, Switzerland and France, where its advantages appear on a larger and more striking scale.

In closing this brief sketch of forest policy in
Prussia, you will perhaps allow me to refer for a moment to the erroneous ideas of German forest management which have crept into our literature. They
have done so, I believe, partly through a desire of
the advocates of forestry to prove too much, and
they injure the cause of forestry, because they tend to
make forest management ridiculous in the eyes of our
citizens. The idea has arisen that German methods
are exaggeratedly artificial and complicated, and not
unaturally the inference has been made that forestry
in itself is a thing for older and more densely populated countries, and that forest management is inap-
plicable and incapable of adaptation to the conditions
under which we live. It is true, on the contrary,
that the treatment of German forests is distinguished
above all things by an elastic adaptability to circumstances, which is totally at variance with the iron-clad

formality which a superficial observation may believe it sees. It is equally true that its methods could not be transported unchanged into our forests without entailing discouragement and failure, just as our methods of lumbering would be disastrous there: but the principles which underlie not only German, but all rational forest management, are true all the world over. It was in accordance with them that the forests of British India were taken in hand and are now being successfully managed, but the methods into which the same principles have developed are as widely dissimilar as the countries in which they are being applied. So forest management in America must be worked out along lines which the conditions of our life will prescribe. It never can be a technical imitation of that of any other country, and a knowledge of forestry abroad will be useful and necessary rather as matter for comparison than as a guide to be blindly obeyed.

It must be suited not only to the peculiarities of our national character, but also to the climate, soil and timber of each locality, to the facilities for transportation, the relations of supply and demand, and the hundred other factors which go to make up the natural character of a hillside, a county, or a State. Its details cannot be laid down *ex cathedra*, but must spring from a thorough acquaintance with the theory of forestry, combined with exhaustive knowledge of local conditions. It will necessarily lose the formality and minuteness which it has acquired in countries of older and denser settlement, and will take on the character of largeness and efficiency, which has placed the methods of American lumbermen, in their own sphere, far beyond all competitors.

All forest management, as contrasted with our present hand-to-mouth system of lumbering, must mean the exchange of larger temporary profits for returns which are indeed smaller, but which, under favorable circumstances, will continue and increase indefinitely.

Under these conditions I do not believe that forest management in the United States will present even serious technical difficulties. It only asks the opportunity to prove itself sound, practical and altogether good.

FRANCE.

In France, which stands with Germany at the head of the nations as regards thoroughness of forest policy, the large extent of government and other public forests is in excellent condition. The struggle for their care and preservation, the necessary antecedent of their present favorable situation, has a history which reaches back far beyond the time when the United States became a nation. Says M. Boppe, in the introduction of his *Traité de Sylviculture*:[1]

"In early times, during the Middle Ages, and until the beginning of modern times, the knowledge of the specialists was summed up in certain practices of lumbering put together in a way to satisfy needs which were purely local. The wood was cut methodically, but without much care as to the manner in which it would grow again; that was the business of Dame Nature. Speaking of France alone, it is known that towards the middle of the sixteenth century, in spite of the fact that lumbering was restricted by limited demand (since, in the absence of the more powerful means of transportation, the wood must be put in use almost where it was felled); in spite of the repeated intervention of royal authority, the lack of foresight and abuses of all sorts resulted in the notable

[1] Paris, 1889.

impoverishment of our forest domain. It was then that a man of genius, Bernard de Palissy, called the carelessness of his times in respect to the forests 'not a mistake, but a calamity and a curse for France.'

"Henry IV made every effort to put an end to the destruction, but it was reserved for Louis XVI, or rather for his minister, Colbert, to reconstruct on a solid basis the foundation of forest ownership. The law of August, 1669, which is in itself a whole forest code, will remain a legislative monument from which we cannot too much draw our inspiration."

The history of forestry in France continued to be associated with illustrious men in more recent times, among whom Recamier, Duhamel and Buffon were the first to "define the first principles of a rational forest management, based on the knowledge which had been gained of vegetable physiology."

France differs from Germany in the unity of her forest law. The Forest Code,[1] which closed in 1827 the series of forest enactments since the time of Colbert, is still in force. Its provisions, altered but little by the political changes which have passed over them, are valid for the whole of France.

In accordance with them certain classes of forest property are to be administered directly by the State forest service, along the lines which it marks out. These are the woods and forests which formed part of the domain of the State, those of communes and sections of communes, those of corporations and public institutions, and finally those in which the State, the communes or the public institutions have joint rights of property with individuals.

The area of forest owned by the French government reaches a total of 2,657,944 acres, or about one-ninth of the whole wooded area, which itself covers 17 per cent. of the country. Considerably more than

---

[1] Consult *Code de la Legislation Forestiere*, per A. Puton, Paris, 1883.

half of the Government forests stand on hilly or mountainous land. The forest administration to which their care is entrusted is attached to the Department of Agriculture, and the Minister of Agriculture is president of the Forest Council. This body includes the Director of the Forests and three administrators, the first of whom is at the head of the Bureau for Legal Matters, Forest Instruction, Records and Acquisitions; the second of the Bureau of Working Plans and Utilization, and the third of that for Reforesting the Mountains, Public Works, Replanting and Clearing.

The personnel under the general direction of this council consists of 36 conservators, who are the higher inspecting and controlling officers; 225 inspectors, who are in administrative charge of divisions called *inspections;* 242 assistant inspectors, the executive officers, each of whom personally directs the work in his *cantonment*, and 328 officers of lower rank, called *gardes généraux*, whose work, in many cases similar to that of the grade above them, is difficult to define. Besides the 834 members of this superior branch of the service, there were in 1885 some 3,532 forest guards of various grades. It is safe to assume that the force of the protective staff has remained substantially the same.

The system of training for the service of the superior staff differs widely from that which we have seen in Germany. There is but one higher forest school, that at Nancy, in place of the numerous institutions of the Germans, and until very recently the whole course of preparation required of candidates for the government service consisted in the two years of study which it offered. At present entrance to the forest school is open only to graduates of an agricultural institute in Paris, but this innovation had its rise rather in political than in educational grounds. The fact remains that the French forester, with a course of training only from a fourth to a third as long as that of his German colleague, has produced results whose admirable educational and intrinsic value stands unquestioned.

All French government forest officers must pass through the school, and the demands of the vast territory under their care are supplied by an annual list of graduates, which does not in general exceed ten or twelve.

Such facts make the task of national forest administration seem lighter as we look forward to the time when it must be begun.

There is a professional school at the Domaine des Barres for men of the higher grade of forest guards who have shown the ability and the ambition to rise to the lower rank of the superior staff. There were last year twelve students in attendance.

The management of the wood lands of communes and public institutions, which cover together an area of 4,715,124 acres, has been already shown to rest with the State forest service. These facts are made the subject of special provisions in the Forest Code, of which the following are the most important:

The communes, corporations and other public bodies may make no clearing in their forests without an express and special permit from the President.

Communal forests can never be divided among the inhabitants.

A quarter of the forests belonging to communes and other public bodies shall always be placed in reserve when these communes or public bodies shall possess at least ten hectares (24.7 acres) of forest.

The choice of forest guards, made by the class of proprietors in question, must be approved by the Government forest service, which issues their commissions to the guards. These last stand in all respects on the same footing as the guards of the State forests.

The sale of wood is made under the direction of the State forest officers, and in the same way as for the State forests. The amount of wood needed for actual use by the members of the community is reserved at the time of sale, and the distribution is made among them with the family as the unit.

In return for a fixed tax all the operations of conservation and management in the woods of communes and public bodies are carried out by the members of the State forest service without further charge.

The object of the reserved quarter (quart en réserve) of the forests of communes and public institutions, mentioned above, is to provide for emergencies and special demands upon the treasury of their proprietors, such as damage by fire or flood, the building of a church, a school-house or a public fountain.

Except when sylvicultural reasons may require it to be cut, such extraordinary necessities alone justify a draught on this simple kind of reserve fund.

The great majority of the forests owned by the class of proprietors just mentioned are managed under the system of "coppice under standards," a name which literally reproduces the French *taillis sous futaie*. This method of handling a forest implies an upper and a lower store of growth. The basis of the treatment is a cutting over of the coppice shoots or sprouts which spring up from the old stumps at regular intervals of from fifteen to forty-five years. In order to make the return annual and fairly uniform it is only necessary to divide the whole forest, if it be small, or each of its units of management, if it be large, into as many compartments of equal productive power as there are years in the rotation of the coppice, and to cut over one such compartment each year.

At each cutting the best of the young seedlings which may have grown up among the coppice, or of the coppice shoots themselves if the seedlings are wanting, are left to grow on for two, three, four or even five rotations of the underwood. Being thus comparatively isolated these standards produce wood very rapidly, while, at the same time, their number is so restricted that they do not seriously interfere with the growth of the coppice by their shade. The disadvantages of the treatment are the large proportion of low-priced firewood which it yields, and the severe demands which it makes upon the soil. But this "national French treatment," as it has been called, has very many qualities which recommend it. It is the form of treatment which yields the highest per cent. of return on the capital invested, as well as the highest absolute volume of wood (if we except the high forest of coniferous trees). According to the forest statistics of 1878, the most recent source of information, the average yield of coppice under standards in France, under State management, was fifty-nine cubic feet of wood per acre per annum, about one-fourth of which was lumber and the rest fuel, hoop-poles, etc. A net annual return of 5 per cent. may be set as the upper limit of production of this class of forest, and therefore far beyond that of other forms of treatment.

In 1878 the average net revenue of all the State forests was 32.00 francs per hectare per annum, or about $2.50 per acre. The return on the capital which they represented was stated at $2\frac{1}{2}$ per cent. As an illustration of the general financial situation of forestry in France, the budget of the forest service for 1891 may be cited. It provides for expenses in the round sum of fifteen and a half million of francs, and anticipates a gross revenue of twenty-five million. If we subtract the cost of re-foresting the mountains, managing the Algerian forests, which, as yet, cost more than twice as much as they bring in, and similar items which are not directly connected with the current expenses of forest management, we reach a total of ten million francs in round numbers. Subtracting similarly the Algerian income we find that the net revenue is expected to reach the sum of fourteen million francs. Forest management on this basis is very far removed from sentimentalism and the philanthropic forest protection whose watchword is "Hands off."

The provisions of the code concerning private wood lands are substantially as follows:

No private owner may root up or clear his wood lands without having made a declaration of his intention at least four months in advance. The forest service may forbid this clearing in case of the maintenance of the forest is deemed necessary upon any of the following grounds:

1. To maintain the soil upon mountains or slopes.

2. To defend the soil against erosion and flooding by rivers, streams or torrents.

3. To insure the existence of springs and watercourses.

4. To protect the dunes and seashore against the erosion of the sea and the encroachment of moving sands.

5. For purposes of military defense.

6. For the public health.

A proprietor who has cleared his forest without permission is subject to a heavy fine, and may be forced in addition to replant the area which he has cleared.

The area of forest in France has certainly passed its lowest point. The following figures, compiled in 1889, will serve to illustrate this statement: No government forests have been sold since 1870, while their area since 1872 has been increased by 190,462 acres. Private owners have been allowed to clear an area amounting to 960,849 acres since 1828, or 10,225 within the last five years, while the clearing of communal forests since 1855 and 1885, respectively, has been 24,826 acres and 598 acres. It should be added that an unknown quantity of land has been cleared without leave, and that on the other hand private owners have been in the habit of getting permits to clear their land as a means of enhancing its selling value and then leaving it still under forest.

Perhaps the most brilliant work of the French foresters has been accomplished in the correction of the torrents in the Alps, Pyrenees and Cevennes, in the course of which over 350,000 acres have been rewooded under difficulties which seem almost insurmountable. Its picturesque character, its thorough success and the sharpness of the moral which it serves to point have rightly made this branch of forestry in France a favorite subject for writers and speakers on forest reform. There is, then, the less need to do more than add that of the total cost to the French government, some 50,000,000 of francs, about one-half was consumed in engineering works whose direct object was to make the replanting of the drainage areas of torrents possible. "The forest thus restored to its natural place is alone able," says M. Demontzey, the eminent French authority, "to maintain the good, but precarious, results of the works of correction in the water-ways themselves." The disappearance of this forest in the first place may be traced in most cases directly to mountain pasturage, and the whole story of *reboisement* in France is full of the deepest interest in comparison with the present state and probable future of our mountain forests.

The planting of the dunes and the Landes, the first of which especially was an achievement of which any nation might well be proud, remain to be mentioned, but the information available to the writer at the moment is neither recent nor complete, and these matters must be left untouched in the present paper.

SWITZERLAND.

I pass now to Switzerland, a country where the development as well as the actual condition of forest policy may well claim our attention. The history of forestry in the Swiss republic is of peculiar interest to the people of the United States, because in its beginnings may be traced many of the charateristics of the situation here and now, and because the Swiss, like the Americans, were confronted by the problem of a concrete forest policy extending over the various states of a common union. The problem has been brilliantly solved, and not the least result of its solution is the fact that the people of Switzerland have recognized the vast significance of the forests in so mountainous a country, and a full and hearty appreciation and support of the forest policy of the Confederation fills every nook and corner of the land.

The history of the forest movement in Switzerland has not yet been fully written, but you will allow me to quote from an unpublished sketch of it by Professor Landolt, who, more than any other man, has contributed to make that history of which he writes. As an example set by a republic to a republic, as the brilliant result of the work of a few devoted men, crowned by a public opinion which they created, and rewarded by the great and lasting blessing which they have brought to their country, I believe that the advocates of forest reform in America can set before themselves no better model and take encouragement from no worthier source.

"Soon after the middle of the last century," begins Professor Landolt, "certain intelligent, public spirited men of Zurich and the canton of Bern (which then included Waadt and a great part of Aargau), turned their attention to the situation of agriculture and forestry in Aargau. Their object was to gain a knowledge of the conditions involved and their surroundings, and to remove the most pressing evils.

"In the years between 1780 and 1790 the cantons, following the lead of Bern, succeeded in appointing forest officers, whose first task was to become conversant with the actual management of the State and large communal forests, and to make suggestions for their future treatment. Partly at this time, partly earlier, a large proportion of the State and a few communal forests were surveyed and a few of them were marked off into compartments on the ground, a measure of vital importance to conservative management.

"The appointment of State forest officers is to be regarded as the beginning of regular forest management. Great numbers of forest regulations bearing on the most various subjects—tree planting among others—had been promulgated in former centuries. They had been often renewed, but without forest officers they could not be enforced.

"Forest regulations were now made by Bern, Zurich, and for the Jura by the bishop of Basel, who also had appointed forest officers.

"The treatment of the State and of a few of the larger communal forests made very satisfactory progress until 1798. Then came the revolution, and with it war and times of great disturbance and political excitement. It is true that even then forestry was never wholly neglected; but the progress made, where it existed at all, was of very minor importance. But as times grew quieter and the condition of the government more orderly, the interest in forest matters revived; the cantons Neuenburg, Freiburg, Solothurn and Aargau passed forest laws of more or less comprehensive scope, appointed forest officers, and in general sought to promote the cause of forestry.

"Until about 1830 forestry in the less mountainous parts of Switzerland developed slowly, but still in a satisfactory manner. New laws appeared, the number of forest officers increased, the wood lands of communes and public institutions attracted more attention, and the future reforesting of the country became gradually the centre of greater effort. In public forests other than those of the State, progress was in general slow, although a considerable number of forest surveys were carried out.

"The mountain forests, however, with few exceptions, were in complete disorder. But the following years brought new life not only into politics, but also into national economies and the status of the forest, which last was materially improved by the floods which spread in 1834 over the greater part of the Alps. The damage which they caused was so severe that the philanthropic and scientific societies set themselves the task of searching out the cause of inundations, which became more frequent as time went on. They concluded that it was to be found largely in the improvident destruction of the mountain forests. To the fear of a wood famine, which had hitherto been the chief incentive to the advancement of forestry, there was now added another, which, if not wholly new, still had been formerly little insisted on. It was the influence of forests on rainfall and the phenomena of nature in general. The societies did not fail to direct attention to this question, and with excellent result. The less mountainous cantons with imperfect legislation made new laws or amended and completed the old ones, saw to the appointment of foresters, and took the organization of the felling, planting and care of their timber seriously in hand. But the chief gain lay in the fact that the mountain cantons applied themselves to the work. St. Gallen, Luzern and Freiburg had already begun, and now went vigorously forward. Graubunden, Tessin and Wallis passed forest laws and appointed forest officers, partly at once, partly later; but still the progress made was slow. The cities everywhere made important contributions toward a better system by the introduction of a wiser treatment and by the appointment of foresters of their own, and so set a good example to the cantons and private forest proprietors. Those cantons of the plains also which had formerly given scant attention to their communal forests, as was here and there the case, now supervised and managed them better.

"Taken as a whole, Forestry has made satisfactory progress as regards legislation, the improvement of forest management and the increased number of forest officers, from the beginning of the 40's on. In 1865 the Swiss Forest School was established (as a fifth department of the Polytechnicum at Zurich), and provision was thus made," says Prof. Landolt, "for a forest staff of our own, educated with special reference to our own conditions.

"The Swiss Forestry Association was founded in 1843. Through frequent agitation, and by setting forth what action was necessary, it has rendered great service to the cause of forest protection. It has moved successfully, among other things, for the foundation of a forest school, the examination of the higher mountain forests, the passage of a new forest law, and the correction of the torrents.

"In 1854," continues Prof. Landolt, "I called the attention of the Association to the investigation of the mountain forests. In 1855 I was entrusted with the preparation of a memorial to the Federal Assembly, which was approved and presented in the following year. In 1858 the Federal Assembly appointed a commission of three men with authority to study and report upon the Swiss Alps and the Jura in regard to geology, forestry and police regulations, bearing on water supply. From the appearance of the final report of this commission in 1861, the improvement of Swiss forestry has been kept steadily before the Confederation. In 1875 a federal forest inspector was appointed, and a year later the first Swiss forest law was passed. This law does not extend to the whole of Switzerland, but only to the Alps and the steeper foot-hills. More recently attempts have been made by the cantonal government and the Forestry Association to extend its influence to the Jura or to the whole of Switzerland, but the need of such action is not yet clearly apparent."

The passage of the federal forest law was followed almost everywhere immediately by the appointment of trained forest officers, and all the cantons whose forest legislation was defective amended or completed it. At the same time federal and cantonal regulations bearing on watercourses were being revised.

"Our forest laws," Prof. Landolt goes on, "are intended to work more through instruction, good example and encouragement than by severe regulations. This method is somewhat slower than one which should involve more drastic measures, but the results achieved are the more useful and lasting. When forest proprietors do something because they are convinced of its utility, it is done well and with an eye to the future; but what they do under compulsion is done carelessly and neglected at the first opportunity. What they have come to learn in this way, and have recognized as good, will be carried out, and that better and better from year to year.

"All our laws require the same treatment for the forests of the State, the communes and public institutions. Still, progress in the treatment of State forests and those of the larger communes is more rapid than in those of corporations and the smaller villages. In the first more money is available, the forest officers are better trained, and there is a more intelligent grasp of the situation. But still the condition of the smaller forests is now satisfactory.

"The oversight of private forests is less strict. Their owners may not reduce the area of their wood lands without the consent of the cantonal government, must plant up the land cut over which is without natural growth, and are bound to take proper care of the growing stock, but they are not held to a conservative management.

"The regulations which bear upon the protection of wood lands, and the harmful external influences to which they are exposed, are equally binding upon them; but in return they enjoy the protection which the law provides for the forest.

"In protection forests, on the other hand, the timber that may be cut by private owners is marked by government officers, so that reckless lumbering may be prevented. The regulations which look to the formation of new protection forests must also be conformed to by private proprietors, or they must allow themselves to be expropriated. In these matters the Confederation and the cantons work in unison. The consent of the Federal Assembly is necessary to the clearing of private land in protection forests."

The Federal forest law, of which Prof. Landolt writes, is binding over nearly two-thirds of all Switzerland. Its chief provisions are the following:

The supervision of the Confederation is exercised, within the forest area over which it has special jurisdiction, upon all protection forests, and furthermore upon all State, communal and corporation wood lands, even when they do not fall under that head.

The cantons must appoint and pay the number of suitably educated foresters necessary for the execution and fulfillment of the forest law.

All forests which fall under Federal supervision must be demarcated on the ground within five years from the passage of the law.

The burdening of the wood lands with new prescriptive rights of certain kinds is forbidden.

The State, communal and corporation forests are to be surveyed, their management regulated, and working plans for them must be drawn up.

The federal machinery for the enforcement of this law is contained in the office of the Inspector-General of Forests, whose sphere of action extends over all the wood lands in question. Each canton has its own forest organization. The Federal Forest School, of which Prof. Landolt was founder, and in which he still teaches the forest sciences, remains in Zurich.

After what has been said it need hardly be added that the forests of Switzerland are for the most part in admirable condition. Systematic forest management has probably been known there as long as anywhere in Europe, and nowhere can finer individual examples be found. I have seen nothing, even in Germany, which seemed to me to be so workmanlike as the management of the Sihlwald, a forest belong-

ing to the city of Zurich; and I am the bolder in my
opinion because the Sihlwald has been called the most
instructive forest of Europe by one who is perhaps
the most experienced forester of the present day. It
may not be out of place to quote certain details of
its history and management from a paper of the
writer's which appeared in *Garden and Forest* in
July and August, 1890.

The ownership of the city of Zurich in its forest
is of very old date. Evidences of the care which
the burghers bestowed upon it are found in a series
of ordinances which, beginning in 1309 with a rule
that no forester might cut wood in the Sihlwald—
clear proof that a forest police existed at that early
date—continued in unbroken succession to that of
1417, under which the foundation of the present
organization was laid, and finally, in 1697, reached
the first technical working plan. It is curious to
note, as an evidence of the view of the nature of its
interest held by the city, that the policy of adding
to the public forest property by purchase, recently
inaugurated by the Legislature of the State of New
York, was begun by the free city of Zurich nearly
two centuries before the discovery of America.

. . . .

"In the organization of a normally stocked forest the object of
first importance is the cutting each year of an amount of timber
equal to the total annual increase over the whole area, and no more.
It is further desirable in any long settled community that the forests be so managed as to yield a measurably constant return in
material. Otherwise difficulties in the supply of labor and the disposal of the produce make themselves felt, and the value of the
forest to its owner tends to decrease.

"In order to attain this steadiness of yield it is obviously necessary that a certain number of trees become fit to cut each year.
The Sihlwald has accordingly been so "regulated" that areas of
equal productive capacity are covered by stocks of every age, from

last year's seedling to the mature tree. These age-gradations succeed each other in a series so regular that in an hour's walk one may pass from the area just cut over through a forest of steadily increasing age to the trees which have reached the limit of the rotation of ninety years. Three such units of management are present in the Sihlwald, but . . . . it will be necessary to speak of only one of them. The working plan for the Lower Sihlwald, then, prescribes for the forest which it controls the operations of what Dr. Schlich has called in his *Manual of Forestry* 'The Shelter-wood Compartment System.' It may not be without interest to follow the life history of a compartment in which this system is carried out.

"After the mature trees had been felled and removed from the area which furnished the yield of the Lower Sihlwald last year the thick crop of seedlings which had grown up under their shelter was finally exposed to the full influence of the light and air. The felling and rough shaping of the timber, the piling of logs and cordwood and the trampling of the men had combined with the crisis of exposure to destroy the new crop in places and create a few small blanks. Here, as soon as the disappearance of the snow had made it possible, groups of the kinds of seedlings necessary to preserve the mixture or destined to increase the proportion of the more valuable species were planted. The operation, necessarily an expensive one, is justified by the greater resistance of a mixed forest to nearly all the calamities which may befall standing timber. Simultaneously with the planting the willows, hazels and other worthless species were destroyed, as well as the 'pre-existing seedlings,' whose larger growth, according to the disputed theory held at the Sihlwald, would damage their younger neighbors more by their shade than their greater volume would increase the final yield of timber. The incipient forest, then, practically uniform in age and size and broken by no blanks which the growth of a year or two will not conceal, is fairly started on the course of healthy development which it is to continue undisturbed until it reaches the age of fifteen years.

"At this point occurs the first of a series of thinnings (or more exactly, 'clearing' at first and thinning later), which follow each other at intervals of seven or eight years, until the trees have entered the last third of their existence. There is, perhaps, no silvicultural question more in dispute than this of the time and degree of thinning which will yield the best results in quality and quantity of timber. The method pursued at the Sihlwald, consecrated by habit and success, gives ample space for the healthy development of the crown from a very early age without admitting light enough through the leaf-canopy to sustain an undergrowth until the trees are nearly ready to give place to their descendants. Such shrubs or seedlings as still appear, thanks to a shade-bearing temperament, are systematically cut out. It may be strongly doubted whether such a policy might safely be applied on soil less moist than that of the Sihlwald; but here, at least, the trees reach the age of sixty years, tall, straight, clean-boled, and in condition to make the best of the last part of the period of maximum growth, which a large number of measurements have shown to occur in general between the ages of seventy and ninety years. A heavy thinning now comes to the assistance of the best specimens of growth, and they are left to profit by it until seven years before the date fixed for their fall. Then begin the regeneration cuttings, whose object is to admit through the leaf-canopy an amount of light, varying with the temperament of each species, whose mission is to give vitality to the seedlings which the trees, stimulated themselves by their more favorable situation, now begin to produce in considerable quantities. To this end the light which falls from above has a powerful auxiliary in that which the system of felling each year in a long, narrow strip admits from the side, and so admirable is this double method that the time which elapses between the beginning and the end of a regeneration is but half the average for less favored localities. This applies only to the deciduous trees. The time required by the conifers is much longer, and the incomplete regeneration which they furnish is supplemented by planting in the blanks already mentioned. But for the self-sown seedlings of both classes the amount of light is gradually increased, the trees which sheltered them are at length wholly removed, and the cycle of growth repeats itself.

"With an average stand of timber of 2,800 cubic feet per acre, the annual yield of wood, almost half of which is from thinnings alone, reached last year 377,023 cubic feet, an amount which may be taken as slightly above the average.

"Under the management of Forstmeister Meister the 2,400 acres of the Sihlwald gave last year (1889) a net return of something over $8 per acre, or a total contribution to the treasury of the city of about $20,000. This sum, large as it is in relation to the area of forest which produced it, promises to be materially increased.

"But with the climate of northern Europe indicated by a mean temperature of forty-eight degrees Fahrenheit, and with the conditions of soil and moisture which it enjoys, the exceptional productiveness of the Sihlwald would still remain partly unexplained were it not possible to add that the land which it covers has been uninterruptedly under forest for something over a thousand years. That precious condition of the surface which the French and Germans unite in describing as 'forest-soil,' so slow in forming and so quick to disappear wherever the full sunlight is allowed to reach the ground, has here been produced in perfection by centuries of forest growth. It is perhaps to this factor, next to the abundance of humidity, that the high annual yield of wood in the Sihlwald is due."

It has been remarked already that there are reasons which give the study of forestry in Switzerland peculiar value—a value which, in the opinion of the writer, far surpasses that of the more refined German forest organization. For the fundamental difference of political training in the German and Swiss forester works itself out in the character of forest management with perfect clearness. "The first," says Forstmeister Meister, one of the most eminent of Swiss or of European forest officers, in summing up the matter to the writer, "has always before his eyes a forest organization regulated down to the minutest detail. It is with this organization that he is to deal as best he may. The Swiss (or the republican) standpoint, on the other hand, requires the forester to reach the best result which is possible at the moment by an intelligent application of the general principles of forestry through the medium of forest organization, which is imperfect and incomplete." It seems hardly necessary to point out along which of these lines the work of the American forester must be shaped, or from which point of view he must approach it. It is an admirable training to become thoroughly at home in the details of the most complete forest organization, but it is a far more practically useful thing in the United States to be able to do without it.

AUSTRALIA.

Before touching on the matter of forest management in certain of the English colonies, it is of interest to note the relations of timber import and export throughout the British Empire. These are given by Dr. Schlich[1] for the average of the five years from 1884-88 as follows:

```
Imports—United Kingdom............£15,000,000
         British Colonies.............  1,466,000
                                       -----------
              Total...................£16,466,000

Exports—Dominion of Canada.........£ 4,025,000
         Other Colonies..............    713,000
                                       -----------
              Total—..................  4,738,000
```
Excess of imports over exports £11,728,000, or $56,800,000.

It should be noted that this table is not quite complete, but it will answer all the purposes of illustration, and the light which it throws on the general timber supply of the world is exceedingly interesting, even if it be not alarming.

Forest legislation in Australia is still in a transition state. It has already had time to correct some of its earlier mistakes, and the course which it is following will certainly lead to a satisfactory forest policy in the end.

In the colony of South Australia an act was passed in 1873 dealing, as such preliminary legislation generally has dealt in recent times, with the encouragement of tree planting. A forest board was established in 1875 and a conservator of forests in 1877; and in 1882 "The Woods and Forest Act" became

---

[1] Lecture before the Royal Colonial Institute on March 11, 1890. My information on the forest policy of the Australian colonies is derived from the same source.

law. It entrusts the charge of all forest estates to the Commissioner of Forest Lands, and gives him power to grant licenses and make regulations for cutting timber, bark, or other forest produce, and he may levy fees upon stock pasturing in forest reserves. It provides also that all forest reserves heretofore declared such shall remain so, and empowers the governor to add to their area; makes provision for encouraging tree-planting, and for the leasing of forest lands under certain conditions. The appointment of conservators is authorized, and the issuance of regulations for the management of the forest, the disposal of the timber, and the prevention of fires. The financial result of this policy during the thirteen years ending with 1889 was a net surplus of over $40,000.

In the colony of New South Wales the forest law dates from 1884, and makes provisions which are partially similar in character to those of the act just mentioned. In accordance with them an area of five and a-half million acres had been declared State forests and timber reserves in 1887.

Victoria, the smallest of the Australian colonies, is perhaps the most interesting from the forester's point of view. From certain reports made to the Secretary of State for the colonies it appears that in the year 1875 Victoria was suffering from a condition of affairs strongly suggestive of our own at present. "The amount of timber is diminishing owing to clearings for settlement, ordinary home consumption and bush (i. e. forest fires). . As early as 1866 attention was called . . . to the wastefulness and improvidence of the prevailing system."

Only the prime parts of trees were utilized. Immense numbers of standing trees were killed, owing to the practice of stripping from them large sheets of bark to cover, perhaps, a mere temporary hut. The committee called attention to the growing scarcity of timber for props for mining purposes and the necessity of measures to secure a permanent supply.

"In 1876 an act was passed, called the State Forest Act, which provided, first, for the appointment of local forest boards, which were to have the care of reserves and other Crown lands; secondly, for the appointment of foresters by local forest boards; and thirdly, for the promulgation by the Governor in Council of regulations prescribing the duties of these boards. In 1884 this act was superseded by a new one, which deals with the formation of State forests and timber reserves and their management, and with the management and disposal of timber and other forest produce not included in the State forests and timber reserves.

"The forests generally are worked under the license system, regulated by rules made under the act. There are licenses for felling, splitting, clearing undergrowth, the erection of saw-mills, grazing, the removal of bark, etc."

Unfortunately, this law, which has much to recommend it. has not resulted as well as was hoped. and the reasons for its failure have been defined as follows:

"The immediate causes of this failure are the bad license system, the ill-arranged classification of State forests, timber reserves and Crown lands, the absence of professional foresters to direct operations, and the neglect to reserve the best natural forests."

Dr. Schlich has formulated the requirements of the situation. as follows: First, the engagement of a thoroughly competent forest expert to be the head of the Victorian Forest Department; secondly, the selection, demarcation and legal formation of a sufficient area of reserved State forest, suitably distributed over the country, systematically managed, and efficiently protected; thirdly, the protection and disposal of forest produce on Crown lands not included in the reserved State forests.

INDIA.

Perhaps the closest analogy to our own conditions in the magnitude of the area to be treated, the difficulties presented by the character of the country and the prevalence of fire, and the nature of the opposition which it encountered, is to be found in the forest administration of India, and that in spite of the tropical climate with which it has to deal. The history of the movement is comparatively fresh, and the fact that many problems remain as yet unsolved will scarcely detract from the interest and sympathy with which we may be led to regard it.

Systematic forest management was begun in India about thirty-five years ago, under difficulties not unlike those which confront us now. An insufficient or a wrong conception of the interests involved, the personal bias of lumbermen, the alternating support and opposition of the men in power, were the chief obstacles with which it had to contend; and against them were pitted the splendid perseverance and magnificent administrative powers of one man. The victory was brilliant, conclusive and lasting, and India has to thank Sir Dietrich Brandis for benefits whose value will go on increasing from age to age.

It is extremely interesting, in view of the beginning of State forest management, which must eventually and ought at once be made in the United States, to note that its success in India, in its early stages, was very largely due to the fact that it furnished a net revenue from the very start.

It is also instructive to recall that a large share of the prosperity of Rangoon, whose merchants protested in 1856 that to restrict the teak lumbering was to destroy the growth of their city, is due to-day to the steady business in this very timber which a conservative forest policy has secured.

"History has proved," says Dr. Schlich,[1] "that the preservation of an appropriate percentage of the area as forests cannot be left to private enterprise in India, so that forest conservancy in that country has for some time past been regarded as a duty of the State.

"Of the total area of government forests, which may perhaps amount to some 70,000,000 of acres, 55,000,000 have been brought under the control of the Forest Department. Of this area 33,000,000 are so-called reserved State forests, that is to say, areas which, under the existing forest law, have been set aside as permanent forest estates, while the remaining 23,000,000 are either protected or so-called unclassed State forests. These areas together comprise about 11 per cent. of the total area of the provinces in which they are situated. Rather more than half the area, or about 6 per cent., are strictly preserved and systematically managed forests."

The formation of these reserved State forests was the first step in systematic forest management, and it was carried out along lines which are typical. The forest areas were first selected, following standards which cannot be enumerated here, then surveyed and demarcated on the ground, and finally established as reserved State forests by an act which provided, first, for the presentation within a certain time of all claims against the State forests as demarcated; secondly, for their hearing and definite settlement; thirdly, that no prescriptive rights could accrue in reserved State forests after their declaration as such under the act; and fourthly, for the special treatment of forest offences.

These forests have been gradually brought under simple but systematic methods of management, which

[1] *Manual of Forestry*, Vol. I, London, 1889.

aim at effective protection, an efficient system of regeneration, and cheap transportation, the whole under well-considered and methodical working plans. The forest staff charged with carrying these plans into effect draws its controlling officers from England. Until quite recently it had been the custom to send the young men selected for the Indian forest service to be educated on the continent of Europe, at first in France and Germany, but more lately altogether at the French school in Nancy. The arrangement was not satisfactory, however, and in 1885 the school at Cooper's Hill, near Windsor, was established as part of the Royal Indian Engineering College. It is an institution whose excellence is directly due to the admirable management of Dr. Schlich, formerly Inspector-General of Forests in India, and now its principal professor of forestry. The course, which in its general features resembles that of other forest schools of similar excellence, has recently been enlarged to cover three years, and includes as its final work an excursion of three months in the forests of the continent of Europe under the guidance of Sir Dietrich Brandis. The writer was fortunate enough to accompany the English students during the last one of these excursions, and can testify to its admirable educational value.

For the executive and protective work it is necessary to employ natives, since they alone are equal to the physical labor in so warm a climate. Their technical education is provided for by the Indian forest school, at Dehra Dun, in connection with which is the Dehra Dun State forest. Quite recently its first working plan has been completed for this forest, and while the management of no one forest can be taken as a type of Indian forestry, it may not be without interest to sketch briefly its chief points. Each of the six ranges which the forest contains is divided into twenty compartments, or, in the Indian terminology, coupes, among which the fellings follow a regular sequence, so that each coupe is cut over once in twenty years. The period of work in each coupe really embraces three years, so that different stages of the operations are going on in three of them at the same time. During the first year the tropical creepers which interfere with the lumbering are cut through, and the trees which are to be taken out are selected, marked with the government hammer and girdled. The trees selected are sal (*shorea robusta*) which are unsound, or which would not improve during the next twenty years, trees of inferior species which will still furnish timber, and trees of other inferior kinds which are injuring by their shade the young sal seedlings. The timber trees which have been marked are sold by auction to a contractor, the unit of sale being the square mile, and are removed during the second year. In the third year the less valuable and the injured trees are cut out, hauled to the roads and sold as firewood. This method of lumbering has rightly been called "improvement felling," since their object is to raise the general condition of the forest rather than to draw from it a large annual revenue at present. For minor forest produce a system of sale by tickets is in force, it is said, with admirable result.

The difficulty of coping with forest fires in India would be notably greater than in the United States were it not for the greater density of the Indian population. The method consists in cutting fire paths through the forest of a width varying up to four hundred feet, removing all combustible matter from them, except the larger trees, and patroling them through the medium of a regular fire organization. All holders of prescriptive rights are bound to assist in the event of fire. At Dehra Dun, for instance, a force of five hundred men is available, and a fire is never allowed to burn for more than a couple of days. Smoking in the forest is strictly forbidden, and the building of fires by camping parties and others is very severely regulated.

The results of this thorough and far-sighted forest policy are conspicuous not only in the great fact that the forests yield, and will permanently yield, the supply of timber and forest produce which the population requires, but also in the beginning which has been made toward regulating the water supply in the mountains, and in the increasing capital value and annual net revenue of the State forests.

"So far," says Dr. Schlich,[1] "the government has good reason to be satisfied with the financial results of its forest administration. The net revenue, after meeting all expenses of the department, has been as follows since 1864, the year in which the department was first established as a general State department:

1864 to 1867.	Average annual net revenue		....	£106,615
1867 to 1872.	"	" "	....	133,929
1872 to 1877.	"	" "	....	212,919
1877 to 1882.	"	" "	....	243,792
1882 to 1887.	"	" "	....	384,752

. . . "There is little doubt, if any, that 25 years hence the net surplus will be four times the present amount if the government of India perseveres in its forest policy as developed in the past. Indeed it would not be going too far to say that the increasing forest revenue bids fair to become a substantial off-set against the expected loss of the opium revenue."

---
[1] Loc. cit.

4

There are two other facts resulting from the foreign policy of India which are of special significance to us as citizens of a country where any interference by the government with private rights would be so vigorously resented, and where private enterprise must consequently play so conspicuous a part. First, a body of efficient and experienced officers of all grades has gradually been formed in the State forests whose services are available for the management of private forests, and of communal forests when the time shall come to form them. Secondly, the example set by the well managed State forests and the steadily increasing revenue which they yield, has induced native and other forest proprietors to imitate the State.

The trained foresters, without whom so laudable a purpose must fail, are at hand, and the whole situation argues most favorably for the future prosperity of the country.

SOUTH AFRICA.

The organization of the Forest Service at the Cape of Good Hope is of comparatively recent date. It consists of one superintendent, three conservators, four assistant conservators, and the necessary staff of forest guards. Practically nothing had been done in the eastern half of the colony when Mr. Hutchins, the present conservator in charge of the Eastern conservancy, was called from India to the Cape. The method which he followed and its results are of interest both from the principles which they embody and from the success of his wise and energetic effort for the protection of the forest in the face of popular and legislative neglect. The system of indiscriminate depredation which is so familiar to us in the United States was in full vogue when he arrived. His first work was to survey the boundary lines of the forest. He then succeeded in getting a bill through the Colonial Parliament, claims against the government forest area as he had surveyed it were heard and decided, and the lines of the State reserve were definitely fixed. He was now ready to regulate the management, which was accomplished on the following basis: The whole area, 150 square miles, was divided into a number of units called series (from a French forest term), and each series was again cut up into forty coupes, in one of which the cutting is localized each year. The system may be called, from a partial translation of its French name, "localized selection." It is a modification of what Dr. Schlich has called "the shelter-wood selection system." The beat of a guard is coextensive with a series, and within this area the felling passes over the same ground once in forty years. The faults of the present selection system are that the per cent. of the valuable timber trees is rapidly diminishing in a country where fire-wood is not saleable, and that it exposes the forest unduly to the attacks of fire, its chief enemy there as here. For these reasons the present treatment is to be gradually converted into regular high forest.

The volume and character of the trees marked to fall in each year are entered in a book, and from it the purchases are made. The buyer presents his felling license to the guard of the coupe in question, and cuts and removes the timber himself.

Excellent results are said to have followed a system of temporary permits to "forest cultivators," who are allowed to take up a certain area of land at the edge of the forest for agricultural purposes. In return, they are responsible for the police of the forest in their vicinity, and any unreported depredations mean to them the loss of their permit. Very often their contract demands the planting of a certain area with oak in lieu of a cash payment of rent.

The English oak and American cottonwood and the *Eucalyptus globulus* are extensively planted throughout the Cape and South Africa generally.

OTHER COUNTRIES.

It has been impossible more than to glance at the chief points of forest policy, in a few of the many lands which teem with interest in this respect. I would gladly have called attention to Austria, where an excellent forest service upholds the general principles which we have seen exemplified elsewhere, and to Italy, where the sale of government forests, forced on the State by the pressure of financial necessity, is beginning to bear evil fruit. A circle of lands around the Mediterranean might have been cited to instance the calamitous results of deforestation, and from some of them still further proof might have been adduced to show at what a cost such errors must be repaired. But the countries which have distanced us on the road toward a rational forest policy might better have claimed our attention.

Without passing out of the limits of Europe, it would have been worth while to glance at Sweden, whose government has recognized its obligations as a forest proprietor, and to Russia, which has recently turned its attention to forest matters, and has passed a law (in 1888), of which the following are the more notable features: Clearing is forbidden in protection forests, and is only permitted in others when its effects "will not be to disturb the suitable relations which should exist between forest and agricultural lands." In standing timber all working which tends "to exhaust the standing crop, prevent the natural regeneration of the forest, and change the areas cut over into wastes" are forbidden. The government prepares working plans of protection forests without cost to their owners, and together with areas which have been replanted, these forests are free from taxes. Finally, private owners are forced to replant areas cut over which are without natural regrowth, and on their failure to do so, the work is carried out by the government foresters at their expense. All this in a country which has still 36 per cent. of wood land left.

Nor is it European nations and white colonists alone who have shown a far more intelligent comprehension of the significance of the forest than the United States. Japan has done so most conspicuously. To quote from Heinrich Semler:

"Japan,[1] whose total area includes in round numbers 94,900,000 acres, possesses forests of 28,700,000 acres in extent. This people furnishes a shining example in the matter of forestry. Even the old feudal lords were penetrated with the value of the wood lands, as they showed by the enactment of vigorous protective laws. When in the recent civil war the government of the Mikado destroyed the feudal system, it declared the forests, as far as they had belonged to the feudal lords, to be the property of the State, and promulgated a forest law which was valid for the whole kingdom. Accordingly the forests of Japan are about equally divided between

---

[1] Semler, Tropische und Nordamerikanische Waldwirtschaft und Holzkunde. Berlin, 1888.

the State and private owners. The former manages its wood lands through a forest service with headquarters at Tokio, where is also the forest school. Founded within the last ten years, the school has an average attendance of about 150, and has quite recently been under the charge of Dr. Mayr, whose work on *The Forests of North America* has made his name familiar to the advocates of forestry in the United States. Only a part of the pupils expect to enter the government service.

"The forest service does not rest satisfied with the present proportion of wood land, but busies itself actively with planting, in connection with which the introduction of foreign species has been attempted.

"There is a notable export of wood from Japan to China, and, on the other hand, an import from North America to Japan; which last, however, the Japanese soon expect to be able to do without."

Dr. Schlich's statement of the destructive tendencies of private forest ownership in India might with equal truth have been made as a general proposition. It is the salient fact which the history of the forests of the earth seems to teach; but nowhere have the proofs of its truth taken such gigantic proportions as in the United States to-day. We are surrounded by the calamitous results of the course that we are now pursuing. In fact, it seems as though there were almost no civilized or semi-civilized country in either hemisphere which cannot stand to us as an example or a warning. To this great truth they bear witness with united voice: The care of the forests is the duty of the nation.

The Present Condition

OF THE

Forests on the Public Lands.

BY

EDWARD A. BOWERS.

The Present Condition of the Forests on the Public Lands.

BY EDWARD A. BOWERS,
Secretary of the American Forestry Association,
(Formerly Inspector of the Public Land Service.)

I shall try to outline what the legal and physical condition of this great and necessary element of our national wealth is at the present time, touching only incidentally upon remedies, as you will hear another upon that subject.

The American Forestry Association must recognize at the outset that little improvement need be expected either in the legal protection or the physical condition of the public forests until there is a radical change in the theory held with respect to public forest lands and a complete revision of existing laws relating to them. On the contrary, we must expect, year by year, to see these forests steadily destroyed and injured to such an extent that their renewal and preservation will become less possible, even with our best efforts, and it may be that over large sections no forest covering can be made to take the place of that which is now being destroyed.

I shall take as my text, therefore, this: *The laws provide neither an adequate method for the protection of the public timber, nor for its disposition in those regions where its proper use is imperative.*

First, what are our existing laws; second, what are the general characteristics of the timber region to which these laws apply; and, third, what is their effect upon the forests?

The foundation of our protective system rests upon an act passed March 1, 1817, which authorized the Secretary of the Navy to reserve lands producing live-oak and red cedar "for the sole purpose of supplying timber for the navy of the United States," and, an extension of this law, made by the passage of the act of March 2, 1831, which provided that if any person should cut live-oak or red cedar trees, or *other timber* from the lands of the United States, for any other purpose than the construction of the navy, such person shall pay a fine not less than triple the value of the timber cut, and be imprisoned for a period not exceeding twelve months. Upon this old law, having the construction of a wooden navy in view, the government of the United States has to-day chiefly to rely in protecting its timber throughout the arid regions of the West, where *none* of the naval timber, which the law had in contemplation, is to be found. Can it be wondered that this act does not meet present conditions?

By the act of June 3, 1878 (20 Stats., 88), timber can be taken from public lands, not subject to entry under any existing laws except for mineral entry, by *bona fide* residents of the Rocky Mountain States and Territories and the two Dakotas. The Land Office regulations in reference to this act provide that such timber cannot be exported, that none less than eight inches in diameter may be cut, and that in cutting the timber must not be wantonly wasted or destroyed.

The timber and stone act, passed the same date,

applies only to the Pacific States and Nevada. Under this act land chiefly valuable for timber and unfit for cultivation if the timber is removed, can be purchased for $2.50 per acre under certain restrictions.

The act of June 15, 1880, permitted timber trespassers to purchase the land on which they had committed their depredations, at the usual price, but as that applies only to trespasses committed prior to March 1, 1879, it is of little importance now.

By the act of March 3, 1875, all land grant and right-of-way railroads are authorized to take timber from the public lands adjacent to their lines, for *construction* purposes only; in addition to which the Denver and Rio Grande railroad has the right to cut also for repairs.

The various appropriation bills, authorizing the employment of special timber agents, by implication recognize their authority to protect the public timber.

The settlement laws, under which a settler may enter lands valuable for timber as well as for agriculture, furnish another means of obtaining title to public timber. None of our timber-bearing lands should be subject to such entry, for reasons that will appear later in this address.

With the exception of the timber culture act, designed to stimulate the planting of small areas of trees upon the treeless plains, the above is the only legislation of consequence affecting the public timber lands, or aiming to promote or preserve forests. In no other way than under some one of the above laws can a citizen of the United States use the public timber.

Of the results of the timber culture act it may be well to point out that of the 38,000,000 acres of public lands entered under it, less than 1,000,000 acres have been patented to the entry-men for compliance with the law. That is, not over 50,000 acres have been successfully covered with young tree plantations.

Before considering the effect of these laws, it may lead to a better comprehension of the subject to outline the general location, character and condition of the public timber lands.

Of all those magnificent forests that covered the fertile lands of the middle West and surrounded the Great Lakes, which were originally the property of the government, almost none belong to it now. For this priceless forest treasure the government received nothing, the land alone being regarded as valuable. These forests were attacked with fire and axe, as obstacles to civilization to be disposed of as rapidly as possible, and the government did not interpose the slightest objection to prevent this destruction.

Here and there in the Southern States there are still considerable timber areas belonging to the United States, but these are relatively unimportant, both in extent and for climatic and other reasons. At present the forest bearing lands of the United States are situated either high up on the sides of the great mountain chains that form the back-bone of the continent, or along the slopes of the northern half of our Pacific Coast. These forests are generally remote from settlement, but are becoming less so every year, as the tide of population sweeps over the west and absorbs vast quantities of the more desirable portions of the public domain.

In their natural conditions these regions differ widely. The central mountain region is arid, containing unknown quantities of mineral wealth, with an inferior quality of forest for lumbering, but absolutely necessary for use locally in the absence of better timber. Owing to the general aridity of this region these forests are invaluable as a cover to the mountains from which the water supply is drawn for the extensive irrigation that now exists on the lower lands. These forests are in much greater danger from fire than are those on the Pacific Slope, where the enormous rainfall protects, and has protected during the centuries of their growth, those wonderful forests. In the Rockies the removal of the forest by cutting or by fire means its destruction in very many cases, as there is not sufficient moisture in the soil and air to induce reforestation by natural methods. On the contrary, along the Pacific Slope, a renewal of the forest cover may be reasonably expected. Thus we see that where our public forests are most needed, both for the actual forest product as well as for climatic and agricultural reasons, they are most likely to be destroyed and most difficult to renew.

The great rainfall of our northwestern Pacific Coast is well known, and the unrivalled timber growing there is world-renowned.

A single tree of the immense fir and cedar varieties in that region is often worth a hundred to a hundred and fifty dollars, and many tracts of a square mile are estimated to contain 100,000,000 feet board measure, worth, in the form of lumber, a million and a half of dollars. The United States must still own many hundreds of square miles, worth for the timber alone $20,000 per square mile. Yet the government sells this land for $2.50 an acre, or at $1,600 per square mile. These lands contain little mineral wealth, but are in some cases valuable for agriculture.

One of the most serious obstacles to be overcome in the arid region is fire. It has been stated that more timber is annually burned in the Rocky Mountain region, where every tree is precious, than is used in five years. I have been told, over and over, by men familiar with the region, that it is useless to try to prevent forest fires there. With this I do not agree. To be sure, the population through those regions is sparse, and cannot be collected so readily to extinguish a forest fire as in more settled localities, but this also is an element of protection, in that there are fewer people to fire the forests. In many places the Rocky Mountains are cleft by steep rocky gorges, which in themselves would form fire-breaks, and a series of safety-lanes could be cut through the mountains, separating the timber into comparatively small bodies, so that the fire in one body could not reach that in any adjacent one. The timber thus cut out to form the safety-lanes might not unreasonably be expected to pay all the costs of carrying out this plan. The lumbermen, of course, in stealing timber, take only the best, and leave large quantities of brush and the poorer portions of the tree to furnish food for the first fire which comes along. The Indians still practice their ancient custom of firing the forests to drive out the game on their hunting expeditions. Before the days of the mill-men, these annual or frequent burnings apparently did not produce serious conflagrations in the forest area; but now, by this combination of wasteful millman and hunting Indian, fires rage every year through large tracts of timber in the

Rocky Mountains, and it is no one's business or interest to prevent and stop these conflagrations when once started.

I recollect one August being in the vicinity of the Bighorn Mountains of Northern Wyoming for several weeks, and as I first approached them nothing could be seen at a great distance but a vast cloud of smoke. During the whole period of my stay there this cloud of smoke hung over the mountains, gradually working its way northward, and thus marking the movement of the fire. No one of the many settlers or inhabitants of the towns in the vicinity of these mountains paid the slightest attention to this fire which was destroying millions of property, and changing the future condition of their water supply, on which the whole region depended for irrigation. Apparently it was a matter of such common occurrence that they took no interest in it.

Then there is no more effective way of concealing the cutting of the better portion of a forest than by firing what is left after the timber depredator has carried off his material.

In 1887 I made as careful an estimate of the loss by fire in the destruction of public timber as the insufficient data obtainable permitted, and placed the annual loss to the government at $8,000,000, in the value of wood-material destroyed. This made no account of the secondary and resultant loss from the destruction of the forest protection by floods, drouth, the ruin of the soil and young forest growth, which, though very great, is immeasurable.

Large areas of the finest pine lands have been disposed of by the government in Minnesota and elsewhere, under the settlement laws. There was no other way by which the timber could be acquired, and so lumbermen hired hundreds of choppers who, in addition to their regular work, were required to enter a tract of 160 acres under the pre-emption or homestead laws, and after a nominal compliance with the law, to deed the land to their employers. After stripping the timber from the land it was abandoned, and over great areas once located for homes one can pass now without finding an occupant, the dead trees and barren stumps or an occasional cabin alone attesting the former occupancy of man. Settlements upon timber lands are rarely made in good faith—that is, to establish a home—because the public lands upon which timber is now growing are almost entirely unfit for agriculture, and the system puts a premium upon perjury and wastefulness. For what desire has such a settler to husband the resources of his land? He wants to cut and sell the best portions of his timber, and be off before his fraud is discovered. Or if he sells, the lumberman who buys pays an entirely inadequate price, so that neither the government nor the settler gets the benefit. This great profit goes into the pockets of the wealthy lumberman, who can afford to waste the poorer portions of the timber, as he has paid a price much below the real value of the timber. If he had to pay the approximate value of the timber, this waste would be materially reduced, and the forest thus far preserved. Even when the land is valuable for agriculture, the pioneer who settles upon it to make a home is eager to remove as soon as possible the forest which for him only cumbers the ground. He wastes thoughtlessly the products of centuries, and rejoices in the fall of every forest monarch. Occasionally it happens that after he has profusely supplied his own needs, he can sell the surplus to some lumberman, and thus prevent its complete waste.

For all of these reasons no timber bearing lands, now the property of the United States, should be subject to entry under settlement laws.

Let us now consider how the laws which I have previously mentioned operate. Under the act of June 3, 1878, applying to Colorado and the Territories, settlers and others were permitted to cut timber for mining and agricultural purposes from *mineral* land. Before cutting timber for local use the settler can hardly be expected to sink a shaft or hire a chemist to determine whether the land is in fact mineral or not. He cuts where most convenient for him, without knowing what the character of the land is, and takes the chance of being prosecuted. Not one acre in thousands throughout the region to which this act applies is known to contain minerals, but it is the only act under which timber may be taken by settlers and miners in this great region. Consequently this whole population is forced to steal one of the necessaries of life. The community has become demoralized with reference to this question. The paramount and absolute necessity to obtain timber for use overrides all considerations of right. To the miner and settler of that region the use of timber from local supplies is as absolutely necessary as the use of the water that flows by him, or of the air that surrounds him, and no plan of management which fails to recognize this necessity can ever hope to be successful. In reference to this the Commissioner of the General Land Office, in his last annual report, says:

"It is useless to enact laws to prohibit the use of an article of absolute necessity, upon a judicious use of which the growth and prosperity of our country largely depend. If the exportation of timber and the destruction of trees and undergrowth upon the mountain slopes can be prevented, and other public timber left free and open to all subject to proper restriction, there will, in my opinion, be far less destruction and waste than is now going on through unlawful appropriation and forest fires.

"The laws now in force are discriminating and unjust. Under them the owner of a mine in Arizona, from which he may be receiving an income of $100 a day, can procure all of the timber necessary in developing and operating said mine from the public mineral lands without cost, except for the felling and removing, while the owner of a farm in Minnesota, upon whose labors we are depending for our daily bread, cannot procure a stick of timber from any public land 'with intent to use or employ the same in any manner whatsoever'—not even to build a fire with which to keep the warmth of life in his body if he be freezing—without violating the law.

"The necessity for a general law to remedy this evil cannot be too strongly urged upon Congress."

The settler, after taking a piece of government land in the vicinity of the mountains, finds immediate use for timber for the construction of his buildings and fences, and he naturally helps himself to whatever he desires. The prospector and miner and the great mining companies have the right to cut timber growing on the mineral lands about them; the railroad supplies itself from the adjacent timber, and the settler can hardly be blamed for doing the same. Oftentimes, as a community of settlers becomes sufficiently large to support it, a small saw-mill springs into being, and the wants of this little community are supplied by the local mill, drawing its timber from the government land without any authority whatever. Both of these classes, the settler and the local mill man, are then criminals under the law, and are also liable in a civil action for damages. The special agents employed by the General Land Office to protect the public domain from timber depredations are supposed to collect such testimony as is necessary to sustain a prosecution, and to superintend this prosecution in behalf of the government, the government being represented by the United States district attorneys. Do I need to tell you that before a local jury such prosecutions almost invariably fail.

The sympathies of the entire community are always with these depredators of the public timber, and quite often the jurors themselves have been freely using such timber. Indeed it is a matter of the greatest difficulty to induce a grand jury to indict persons who have confessedly been cutting government timber for years to supply their saw-mills, the product of which is used quite likely by the very members of the grand jury. In the rare cases where a verdict for damages is rendered for the government it will be for merely nominal damages.

"In nearly every public land State and Territory, poor hardworking laboring men, who have been compelled to cut timber to procure the means of a bare subsistence for themselves and families, have been arrested, convicted, fined and imprisoned for cutting and removing timber from vacant, unappropriated and unreserved non-mineral public land in violation of section 2461, U. S. Revised Statutes."

"It is true that in some localities the sympathies of the people are so strong and in other localities the timber is an article of such public necessity, that it is impossible to convict a man for violation of said section, even if caught in the very act and the proof is overwhelming; so that to some minds the retention of that law upon our statutes is deemed quite immaterial." (Commissioner's Report, G. L. O., 1890.)

As conclusive of the futility of the present system, I need only to tell you that during the seven years from 1881 to 1887, inclusive, the value of the timber reported stolen from the government land was $36,719,935, and the amount recovered was $478,073.

The cost of this service for the special agents alone was $455,000. To this expense must be added all of the costs of the trial, such as the District Attorney's and witnesses' fees.

In the Annual Report of 1890, the Commissioner of the General Land Office says:

"A careful examination has been recently made of the annual reports of this office, covering the years from July 1st, 1881, to June 30th, 1889, inclusive, for the purpose of ascertaining what has been accomplished during that time, through legal proceedings, in the way of enforcing the laws for the protection of public timber. The result of that examination is conclusive upon two points:

"First. That the most valuable timber on the public lands is being rapidly exhausted.

"Second. That the several laws relating to public timber now in force are utterly inadequate to properly protect either the public forests from unlawful appropriation or the interests of the settlers engaged in developing the country, to whom the use, to a certain extent, of public timber is essential."

During the past year, in the protection of public timber, fifty-five timber agents were employed, whose services were of such irregular and brief periods as to equal only the employment of twenty-nine agents for one year. These special agents reported 310 cases of timber trespass, involving public timber and its products valued at something over $3,000,000. The government recovered only, from settlements of suits, through legal proceedings and by sales of timber and lumber, $100,940.32. On July 1st, 1890, there were 282 civil suits pending for the recovery of approximately $14,800,000, for timber reported to have been unlawfully cut from the public land, and 306 criminal prosecutions for violation of the timber laws were also pending. The effect of this system has been to place almost the entire population in opposition to the government in its efforts to protect the public timber, and it is all the more difficult now to gain their coöperation. It will be necessary to educate the people up to the belief that this legislation for the protection of public timber is for their benefit, and for their children's, that it is to preserve their country, and to prevent its becoming an arid waste. To attempt a harsh and stringent punishment of unintentional offenders will be to arouse the hostility of all the inhabitants, and probably lead to acts of revenge in firing the forests that would do incalculable harm.

The railroads have cut timber right and left to meet their requirements, and many of them under their charter rights had such privileges in the matter of cutting timber for the construction of the line that it is difficult to determine whether their cutting has been lawfully or unlawfully done. Along those lines of road which had alternate sections of government land granted them, where these lands are unsurveyed, it is, of course, impossible to say whether the land on which the railroad employés are cutting is a section granted to the railroad or a section reserved by the government. The Supreme Court has held that these grants of land are grants *in present;* and that the title to lands so granted vests at once in the railroad upon its fulfilling the conditions of the grant—that is, when it is constructed. That these lands are unsurveyed is not the fault of the railroads—they could not survey them, in any event—consequently the government cannot complain if they continue their cutting in unsurveyed regions. For this reason a large amount of cutting is done at the present time, which may or may not be legal; it is impossible to say.

One of the difficulties in effecting the conviction of timber thieves is the difficulty of placing the responsibility upon the right man. Oftentimes a band of irresponsible foreigners, who scarcely speak the language, will go into the mountains to cut ties for a railroad, for which the railroad is to pay when delivered at certain points on its line. The ties are cut and perhaps are in condition to be floated down to the railroad. Information comes to some government timber agent of this cutting, and he goes to the scene of it. Upon his arrival he finds that the men who cut it are mere employés, and that the responsible parties have decamped, in anticipation of his presence. There are no written contracts, and it is not possible to show the connection between the cutting and the railroad. The railroad has not yet received or paid for the ties. All the agent can do is to seize them, which he does, to find that his only customer is the same railroad that is really responsible for the cutting, and the chances are that he gets a much less price for them than the men who cut them had contracted for, so that his action inures to the benefit of the railroad that ought to be punished. The poor tie-cutters, who have been hard at work in the woods, perhaps for weeks, are the sufferers, losing all their wages; oftentimes without knowing that they had not a perfect right to cut the timber which they were engaged to do by the agent of the railroad. It is manifest from what has been said before, that no local jury would convict these men criminally, or bring a verdict against them for damages.

That this condition of affairs is not the fault of the General Land Office, which has charge of the public timber lands, is evident from the fact that ever since 1879 the Public Land Commissioners and the Secretaries of the Interior have, in annual report after annual report, called attention to their impotence in the matter of protecting government timber, and asked Congress repeatedly for such legislation as would remove this stain upon their administration. Notwithstanding these earnest appeals Congress fails to take any action. The annual appropriation for protective service has been hardly sufficient to keep an average of twenty-five timber agents in the field, and they were supposed to cover and protect 70,000,000 acres of public timber lands. These figures show the utter absurdity of the prevailing system. The officers in charge of the work seemed to have despaired of accomplishing any really beneficial results, and so these places have come to be regarded as political spoils to be distributed among faithful party workers, who, in accepting them, do so with the idea that they are to have a sinecure. The character of the men appointed in this way you can readily imagine. I have seen men sent from cities to superintend the protection of the public forests who probably had never before seen a forest, who were totally unfamiliar with methods of lumbering or estimating the damage done by the cutting of an area of timber, who were not lawyers, and who had no ability whatever to collect testimony on which the district attorney could successfully prosecute.

Many of the honest timber agents find themselves unfit for the work, but have not the frankness to admit it, or the wisdom to resign. Of the dishonest ones, of whom there are too many, I need only say that their position offers them many chances for blackmail, to which the mill-men will submit rather than undergo the cost and anxiety of prosecutions, although they may feel that the prosecutions will be fruitless. A mill-man complained to me on one occasion, that he had no objection to there being a timber agent in the country, as he had found it a cheap way of securing protection, but that recently there had been so many changes made in timber agents that he began to find it too expensive.

The call for some legislation by which timber can be honestly cut from the public lands and paid for is earnest among the mill-men supplying the local demands for lumber in the arid region.

On the Pacific Coast the conditions are entirely different. There the timber is cut principally for export, and not for local use. Unquestionably the finest body of timber anywhere now existing in the United States lies between the Coast Range and the Pacific Ocean, and there milling is pursued on such a large scale that the comparatively small methods of the Rocky Mountain region would not meet their requirements. So, in 1878, what is known as the timber and stone act was passed. By means of this any citizen of the United States, or head of a family, can take up 160 acres of timber land, and by paying $2.50 for it obtain title to the land. There was some attempt in the act to limit its operations by requiring that the would-be purchaser should make affidavit that the land was entered exclusively for his own use and benefit, and by not allowing any association of individuals to enter more than 160 acres, nor could any member of such association make an individual entry. But under this act a very large percentage of the entries made have been made by laborers in the employ of mill companies for those companies, and in one case which came under my observation it was the practice of a lumber company to hire the entire crew of any vessel which might happen to touch at any port to enter pieces of timber land and deed them to the company at once, the company paying all expenses and giving the entryman $50 for his trouble. By such methods have our unequalled red-wood forests been absorbed by foreign and resident capitalists.

From this statement of the condition of the public timber lands of the United States but one conclusion can be drawn: that is, a new departure in the management by the government of its forest property is *imperative*. The time now seems ripe for the introduction of some intelligent policy in the management of our public timber lands. Some of the very men who have been the devastators of our finest forests begin to see the folly of their course, and fear that soon there will be no material for the lumber trade. They are ready and willing to pay the government a reasonable price for timber which can be properly sold. and aver that some system by which they can cut under authority of law is a necessity, being desirous of doing away with the subterfuges of the past. The more intelligent pioneers of the arid regions realize that the regular flow of the streams throughout the whole season. furnishing the water for irrigation through the summer drouth, is changing into torrents of a few weeks' duration in the spring, which carry destruction by their flood and wash away the more fertile soils, and then subside and disappear when most needed. When settlers, lumbermen and miners alike call out for reform, what opposition need we expect? What is to be overcome but the *vis inertiæ* that stands in the way of all reform? One or two cannot accomplish the result which we all desire. Of one thing be assured, only by constant agitation can there be effected a more thorough appreciation by the people of the whole country of the perilous condition of our forests and what their destruction means to our national prosperity. From this alone will remedial legislation spring.

Practicability

OF AN

American Forest Administration.

BY

B. E. FERNOW.

Practicability of an American Forest Administration.

BY B. E. FERNOW,
Chief of Forestry Division, Department of Agriculture, Washington, D. C.

The title of the paper assigned to me should have been made, by preference, to read: "The difficulties attending the introduction of forest management in the United States," for the negative elements in the problem are still so numerous as to make a positive result. at first sight, at least, doubtful.

If we can understand the reasons for the absence of forest management in the United States, we shall at once understand some of the difficulties retarding its introduction and be able to weigh the possibilities of overcoming them.

In Europe, thanks to a certain feudal conservative system, large forest areas were preserved, more or less intact, in strong, controlling hands, until the territory was gradually covered by a dense, stable population, which necessitated conservative utilization of all resources and careful adjustment of private and communal interests.

In this country, on the other hand, a small but energetic and progressive population took possession of and spread itself over an immense territory, boundless in resources, with no check, borne by historical and economic development, which would restrict expansive and favor intensive management of resources.

As is natural under such conditions, individualism has developed itself in proportion to opportunities for its expansion—individual interests and rights are considered foremost, while, with a more or less unstable population, communal interests are but imperfectly recognized and considered, and communal spirit hardly awakened because less necessary.

It is relative density of population, then, which accounts largely for the many differences, social and economical, between the Old and New Worlds, and most certainly for the difference in the use of all resources, the forest resource included.

Private interest in natural resources is concentrated upon present gain, and where this gain can be secured by utilizing only the best of the natural growth, then abandoning the old and opening up a new field, the incentive to management of the resource for continuity is absent.

We may then say that in the United States the absence of forest management from considerations of private interest is due to the fact that there is still a large area of virgin timber left, which can be worked advantageously for present gain by simply utilizing the best natural growth without the necessity of economical management.

That this state of affairs may change in a few decades is no consideration for the present workers of the resource. Their interest lies only in the immediate present, while forest management means curtailment of present revenue for the sake of continued future returns or benefits.

There are some localities in the United States, and some conditions where even now forest management from private considerations is practicable, i. e., profitable, namely, such as are situated with reference to the markets favorably enough to be able, in spite of the increased cost of management, to compete with the virgin supplies shipped from more distant resources, and where density of population permits a fuller profitable utilization of inferior material.

For instance in the Adirondack region, with large, compact holdings, tolerably well stocked and easily made accessible to market, it could be shown that increased profits would result from rational forest management.

Some minor difficulties which would have to be overcome in introducing private forest management, among which the momentum of habit is perhaps the greatest, I may not discuss here.

While, then, the introduction of private forest management, which is based upon considerations of profit, depends almost entirely upon the progress of general development, which we cannot control, there are communal interests involved in the management of certain parts, at least, of the forest areas which make it necessary to weigh considerations of present as against future and continued advantages; to weigh direct value as against indirect value, of the forest resources.

It has been shown, over and over again, that one incontrovertible influence of forest cover exists, namely, upon the regularity of water-flow and soil conditions of mountainous territory; that, therefore, in such territory utilization of existing forest resources must be carried on in such a manner that the forest cover be not interrupted and be reproduced as part of it is removed, if we regard the interests which are dependent upon the existence of the forest cover.

Under such conditions it is quite evident that the community must step in to guard against a destruction of the forest cover. This can be done either by controlling private owners in the use of their property or by placing such areas under a government administration.

The first method is not only unsatisfactory and distasteful, but as it means reduction of private gain, unjust; and, hence, except in special cases, the object would be only partially attained.

We are then driven to consider the second alternative, namely, communal ownership and administration of such areas, which alone insures permanency.

In such an administration the primary consideration, it stands to reason, is not the direct profitableness of the management, but the most economical attainment of the object for which the administration was undertaken, namely, to insure a continuous forest cover.

The consideration of the practicability of such forest management then may be confined to a discussion of the administrative features and the possibility of securing the object in view, while yet satisfying other demands upon the forest cover.

There are, in every State in the Union almost, forest areas which an intelligent communal policy would place under communal administration; but there is, perhaps, no part of the country more in need of immediate government action than those western mountain States in which the larger part is still in the hands of the United States Government.

What the present conditions of this government property are has been fully explained by Mr. Bowers, who speaks from intimate knowledge, and may be found more detailed in various reports of the Departments of the Interior and of Agriculture.

Considered merely as a piece of property, without more than ordinary value, the manner in which it is needlessly wasted without benefit to any one, would stamp its present administration as the most impractical of which thinking man is capable, if "practical" means that which can be done with good reason and to some useful end, that which a practical man would do with his property. It is inconceivable how any management could be more puerile, more devoid of good sense, more absolutely in defiance of all reason and demands of statesmanship, than the present management of the public timber lands.

For not only is this property not protected against theft and fire, but by incongruous, shortsighted and unjust regulations, these two destructive agencies are especially invited and the resident population is forced to resort to theft and fraud in order to supply their present wants, at the same time endangering their future needs and interests.

Any practical and practicable administration of these lands must keep in view not only the peculiar natural condition of these forests, but also the peculiar social conditions of the communities adjoining them. The problem to be solved by such an administration is, while insuring protection against fire and illegitimate use, to provide for the satisfaction of the legitimate wants of different classes of population in the simplest manner without impairing the continuity of forest cover and of reforestation.

In the Fiftieth Congress a bill (H. R. 6045) was introduced, which proposed and outlined in full detail the working of a forest administration for the United States Government timber lands. To see whether and how far such an administration is practicable, it might be best to scrutinize the provisions of this bill. These are briefly as follows:

1. The temporary withdrawal of all timbered land from private entry, and the reservation, after examination, of the areas which are not agriculturally useful, and which ought to be kept in forest growth.

2. The districting of the reserved area and the organization of a force for its administration, which comprises—

(*a*) A central directive office consisting of a commissioner and four assistant commissioners, in either the Department of the Interior or of Agriculture.

(*b*) As many local resident managers or inspectors as there are districts.

(*c*) A force of guards or rangers to protect the property against fire and theft, and to supervise the cutting of timber.

3. Regulations under which wood supplies are to be obtained, under licenses, which take due regard of the different needs of the resident population.

4. Such penal provisions as will make the execution of the administration effective. These will have to be altered to suit the new conditions, due to the creation of new States, by which the United States have lost the right of penal legislation on most of this territory.

The objections made against such legislation may be divided into those which flow from private interest, and those which concern themselves with the principles involved and the practicability of the proposed plan.

The first class of objectors we may dismiss by merely mentioning them; they are those who carry on a nefarious trade without legal status, which would be stopped by a proper surveillance. Unfortunately their cries "that the rights of the pioneers would be curtailed and the development of the country impeded by such a system as that proposed, and that nothing practical could be done to preserve the forest areas," are sufficiently boisterous to influence legislators against change of existing conditions; and while we may neglect them in this discussion, they are an important factor not to be underrated when the passage of such legislation is attempted.

All fair-minded citizens of the West will be found of one opinion, namely, that existing conditions are not desirable and ought to be remedied.

The first objection, based upon principle, comes from the believers in unrestricted individualism. They object to the holding of the land by the government. They contend that such timber lands are in better hands, and will be taken care of more easily and efficiently by private holders, and should be disposed of to them. While this position may be correct as regards other classes of lands and under stable conditions of society, experience has proven it wrong under our conditions, and especially with timber lands.

It is well known that agriculture is carried on in the United States without system or regard to continued fertility in those parts of the country where a thin population permits easy territorial expansion of the individual; that is to say, the ground is worked for what it will yield in the natural state and then abandoned for new fields. But agricultural soils are easily recuperated, while impairing the forest cover on steep mountain sides, especially in such dry regions as we have in the West, which are not readily reforested by nature, imperils far-reaching interests forever, as Europeans have learned to their cost.

Furthermore, timber lands have been and are being disposed of to private individuals on the Pacific Coast, and the consequences are as disastrous and unsatisfactory as they have been elsewhere.

It is also well known that in all parts of the country where timber land and non-agricultural soil is sold to individuals it relapses to the State for non-payment of taxes; for with the valuable timber taken from the tracts the interest of the individual is gone in this kind of property.

But the interest which the community has in the forest cover, especially in mountain regions, is transcendant, for the protection of the forest cover is of importance to the continued welfare of the community, and hence the State, which is not only the representative of communal interests as against individual interests, but also of future interests as against present, can alone be trusted with the ownership of such lands.

The objection to government holding is good only as long as the government does not take proper care of its holdings, as at present; but this is the very thing to be remedied by the proposed legislation.

It might still be asked what part of the community had best be intrusted with the care of these lands, whether it should be the county, the individual, State or the general government.

It may be argued that the community making up the county has necessarily the most interest in the preservation of favorable conditions and can best guard its own interests. Yet there are often conflicts of interests arising which can be better adjusted under State ownership, and before a well settled county administration exists State ownership would be preferable.

But even State ownership, while perhaps desirable at a certain stage of development would not be expedient now, and ownership by the general government for the present is preferable.

My reasons for this preference are:

First. The general government does own the lands, and the difficulties and complications attendant upon wholesale transfer of the property can as well be avoided. If such transfer were to be effected it would necessitate almost a revolutionary change of the existing land policy of the government, which at present seems neither necessary nor advisable.

Second. The States with a scanty population as yet, and with all parts of their economy still to build up, had better not burden themselves with this additional duty of forest conservation, except so far as they can aid it without cost to them.

Other political considerations, which need not be elaborated here, lead to the same conclusions; so that altogether the expediency of retaining the public timber lands in the hands of the general government for the present is conceded by the unbiased students of the question, provided the general government will do what is necessary to preserve and keep in permanent forest condition this property.

If we agree that the administration of these lands is best left to the present owner of them, namely, the United States Government, the next question concerns practicable methods in their administration.

The first need is a proper classification of the remaining public lands, and the withdrawal from entry and permanent reservation of the forest lands.

The withdrawal of these lands might be done by gradual reservations of single parks, of which we have several—based, however, upon other considerations, than those of a rational forest policy—but if the withdrawal is deemed necessary at all it would be wiser to reserve all that is necessary and desirable to reserve at once, while still in the hands of the government and not entirely devastated.

The practical method of withdrawing the lands to be reserved is one of gradual exclusion, requiring those entering public lands for occupancy under homestead and other laws, to make affidavit to the effect that the lands so entered are chiefly valuable for agricultural pursuits, and not for the timber mainly. Meanwhile examination of all entries so made as well as of unentered sections, will gradually make known the character of the land and furnish a basis for the determination of the extent of the reserve. The final survey of these lands also can be made gradually and without much extra expense.

There is next to be provided:

1. Protection against fire over a large mountainous territory, with a scattered population, more difficult because of the coniferous growth and dry climate.

2. Means of supplying wood material for the various needs of the population in a legal manner and in such a way as not to destroy the forest cover.

3. Reforestation, if possible, by natural seeding and recuperation of the areas which have been despoiled so far.

Fire is the great bane of American forests. These conflagrations are due largely to bad habits and loose morals; hence it will not be possible to stop them altogether and at once. But it is practicable to reduce them in frequency and extent. This cannot, however, be done by paper legislation, but only by proper policing. For this it is necessary to divide the territory into districts of suitable sizes, differing according to local, social and topographical conditions; to have officers each in charge of one district and responsible for its protection; to have these officers clothed with sheriffs' power, and in every way capacitated to enforce regulations, apprehend and at once bring to court offenders, and shorten the processes of legal procedure in cases where *prima facie* evidence is at hand.

As we do not expect to have every thief prevented or caught, we cannot expect to have every fire prevented or incendiary apprehended.

But with a responsible guard for a given district, always on the alert, fires will be discovered early after they are started, and be confined, and put out.

To assist in confining fires, it is also proposed to burn over safety strips at the proper season, so that any running fires will be checked and a chance given to fight the fires from these safety strips as a basis.

In regard to the methods of supplying wood material, it is to be kept in view that, in a country which is as yet partially settled and developed, requirements are of a different nature from those of the more densely populated Eastern States. This has been recognized by devising different classes of licenses under which timber supplies may be obtained, namely, one for the settler and one for the prospector, each to supply his immediate wants on a designated area upon payment of a small annual fee, and a further license to the local lumberman, who supplies the smaller communities, upon payment of additional acreage and stumpage fees.

To satisfy the requirements of the lumber business, a business which must exist in every developed community, special licenses are provided, to cover larger areas, with a longer time for cutting, with higher acreage and stumpage fees, and other necessary restrictions and regulations.

It may be stated in passing, that this system of selling stumpage and allowing the cutting by the purchaser, under control, is not the most desirable, and is one to be gradually changed as changing conditions permit, but it seems to be the only practicable one under present conditions.

The third object to be attained by the proposed administration, namely, natural reforestation, and continuity of forest cover, is the only one in which forestry as a science is involved.

To discuss what should or should not be done in this direction, would mean a discussion of the principles upon which technical forest management is carried on. This would lead too far.

I can only say that this object is attained mainly by the manner in which the cutting is done, but it cannot be accomplished by following the simple popular direction to cut the ripe timber.

This is a matter which cannot be determined either by the legislator or the professor *ex cathedra*, a matter that requires a different answer for different conditions, which cannot be given from intuition, but must be evolved from experience. And since the cutting is to be done by licensees, who must be controlled in the manner of cutting, in order to insure proper reforestation, we see at once that here we have reached the real difficulty of the problem, namely, the difficulty of finding the men who combine with the needful organizing and administrative faculties sufficient knowledge of forestry matters to undertake the direction of a forest administration. *In fact, the whole difficulty is one of men, rather than of measures,* and, if it were expected to create all at once a fully developed forest administration, this difficulty would appear almost insurmountable.

Such expectations can rarely be realized in human affairs, and in the proposed forest administration we will also have to be satisfied to find our way through mistakes and partial failure to improved methods, at least, in the technical part of the administration.

So little knowledge of forestry matters exists in this country that it will be utterly impossible to expect such from the many forest guards to be employed. Nor will it be possible to command district officers, with more than the teachings of woodcraft from the lumber camp, yet capable of learning forestry principles. But the directive administration should command experts capable of preventing, from the start, misdirection in technical detail, and of evolving in time a suitable system of forest management, gradually educating the whole force to its teachings. Such expert advisers, if they cannot be found in this country, can be had abroad, and some will be found among us here by the time they are needed.

There is one other objection to the practicability of the proposed administration urged on the score, not of measures, but of men.

Here, again, we can discern between the real and the imagined difficulty.

To do efficient service—and none other is desirable—I estimate that for, say, 50,000,000 acres of government timber lands, from one to two thousand active, reliable guards, and 500 resident managers, all men of special capacity and sound judgment, are necessary. Can they be found? I believe that, if paid in proportion to the service rendered, and not, as is the rule with government service in general, expected to be satisfied with eking out their income by outside work and incidental favors, they can be found.

The imagined difficulty, and the objection raised upon it, comes from those who imagine the government as something outside and inimical to themselves, and every government officer a leech upon the public treasury, an obstacle between themselves and their individual happiness, an element of friction. For a self-governing American, such objection, while containing an element of truth, seems rather morbid and puerile, and is really directed, not against a possible forest administration, but against existing methods of filling offices. As long as offices are filled for political favors, held as temporary make-shifts, bringing neither honor, adequate pay nor assurance of continuity, this objection may not be without foundation, but it is hoped that the spirit of reform may have gathered strength enough to change conditions by the time this administration is to be organized.

To meet any objections against the practicability of such an administration on the score of expense, a rough consideration of this question, based, to be sure, on slender facts, may be in place: Allowing 50,000,000 acres of timber land reserved, I find that a tolerably efficient administration may be provided for a round $2,500,000, or five cents per acre.

It would be satisfactory, of course, if only this expense be covered by the revenue. While the annual growth of wood per acre on the reserved area would exceed in value the assumed cost of administration, the consumption is restricted. But when we consider that the present saw-mill capacity of the region affected is over three billion feet B. M., and the resident population three million, requiring at least fifty cubic feet of wood material per capita, sufficient margin is assured even if only half of these amounts are furnished from the government timber lands.

While, then, from a business point of view a national forest administration is entirely practicable, from a governmental and legislative point of view such difficulties exist as withdraw themselves from the discussion of the uninitiated. Personal considerations and considerations of expediency offer such obstacles to the enactment of thorough legislation as that proposed, that there is but little hope for it.

It takes a giant, or rather two giants combined, strengthened by the courage of conviction that this is an urgent matter to be acted upon, to carry through the flood of legislative streams any measure involving radical changes in the existing land policy. It is the tremendous momentum of bad habits, unfair usage, and personal politics, that must be overcome, to make a rational forest policy possible.

APPENDIX.

PROPOSED BILL.

For the Protection and Administration of Forests on the Public Domain.

DESIGNATION OF FOREST LANDS.

SECTION 1. *Be it enacted by the Senate and House of Representatives of the United States of America in Congress assembled,* That all lands now owned or controlled, or which may be hereafter owned or controlled by the United States, and which are now or shall hereafter be devoted to forest uses, are, for the purposes of this act, declared to be public forest lands.

WITHDRAWAL OF FOREST LANDS FROM ENTRY.

SEC. 2. That the unsurveyed public lands of the United States, embracing natural forests, or which are less valuable for agricultural than for forest purposes, and all public lands returned by the public surveys as timber lands, shall be, and the same are hereby, withdrawn from survey, sale, entry or disposal under existing laws, and shall be disposed of only as provided in this act, and as Congress may hereafter prescribe.

PREVENTING ENTRIES UPON FOREST LANDS.

SEC. 3. That every person applying to make an entry or filing of public lands under any law of the United States before the classification and survey of the public forest lands, as provided in this act, shall be made, shall file with his application an affidavit, under oath, corroborated by witnesses, stating that the land applied for is not exclusively or mainly forest land, is not situated near the headwaters of any stream, and is more valuable for agricultural or mining purposes than for the timber growing thereon, and each such applicant shall state particularly his means of information and his personal knowledge of the facts to which he testifies, and upon a certificate from the Commissioner of Forests constituted by this act the lands so entered may be disposed of under existing laws; and every person swearing falsely to any such affidavit shall be deemed guilty of perjury and liable to the penalties thereof; and all illegal entries of timber lands shall be absolutely void, and, upon satisfactory proof, shall be subject to summary cancellation by the Commissioner of the General Land Office.

INSTITUTING A COMMISSIONER OF FORESTS.

SEC. 4. That there shall be in the Department of the Interior (or Agriculture) a Commissioner of Forests, who shall be appointed by the President, by and with the advice and consent of the Senate; and shall have the care, management and control of all the forest lands owned or controlled by the United States. He shall be a suitable person, versed in matters of forestry, and shall be entitled to a salary of five thousand dollars a year, with such allowances for assistance and expenses as will insure a proper execution of the provisions of this act, and as Congress may from year to year provide. Before entering upon his duties he shall give bonds with sureties to the Treasurer of the United States in the sum of fifty thousand dollars, conditioned to render a true and faithful account to the Treasurer, quarterly, of all moneys which shall be received or expended by him by virtue of the said office.

APPOINTMENT OF FOUR ASSISTANT COMMISSIONERS.

SEC. 5. That the President shall also appoint four Assistant Commissioners. The Assistant Commissioners shall act as a forestry board or council to the Commissioner of Forests in all matters pertaining to the administration of public forest lands, as provided for by this act, and each shall have special charge of one division of the forest reserves, which he shall personally inspect at least once every year. Each of the Assistant Commissioners shall receive a salary of three thousand dollars.

CLASSIFICATION OF FOREST LANDS.

SEC. 6. That the forest lands on the public domain shall be arranged in three general classes, namely: First, lands distant from the headwaters of important streams, covered by timber of commercial value, more valuable for forest purposes than for cultivation; second, lands partially or wholly covered by timber, but suitable for homesteads and more valuable for agricultural purposes than for timber; third, mountainous and other wood lands, which, for climatic, economic, or public reasons, should be held permanently as forest reserves.

ESTABLISHMENT OF FOREST RESERVES.

SEC. 7. That it shall be the duty of the Commissioner of Forests to examine and classify, with the advice and assistance of the forestry board, the forests and public timber lands of the United States, and to determine, subject to the approval of the Secretary of the Interior, what portions of such forests and timber lands should be permanently retained in reservations for climatic or other economic or public reasons, and what portions may be disposed of without disadvantage to the public interests. He shall cause to be prepared connected maps or diagrams showing the approximate situation and areas of public timber lands in each State and Territory, and the President shall, by proclamation, designate the permanent forest reserves as the same shall be selected and approved as herein provided; and it shall be the duty of the Secretary of the Interior to cause exterior boundary lines thereof to be run and marked by durable monuments; and no further survey of any timber lands of the United States shall be made until the permanent reservations herein provided for are established.

RESTORING FOREST LANDS.

SEC. 8. That lands of the second class, when reported to the Secretary of the Interior by the Commissioner of Forests, shall be restored to homestead entry or sale; but a special appraised price of the timber thereon shall be paid by the person entering such lands in addition to the usual price and fees for the land, provided that the timber of five acres shall be allowed to the applicant free of further charge, on the payment of the settler's license fee of two dollars, as hereinafter set forth, and provided also that at least five acres of land shall be cleared and put into crops within one year from the time when a grant shall be made to the applicant, and that a habitable dwelling be erected thereon within one year.

DISPOSAL OF TIMBER.

SEC. 9. That the timber on the lands of the first and third classes shall be disposed of according to the regulations of this act as hereinafter provided.

DOMESTIC LICENSES.

SEC. 10. That the disposal of timber for domestic purposes shall be made by means of licenses as follows, namely: First, a prospector's license shall be granted to any applicant by the local (district) inspector upon the payment of two dollars. Such license shall confer the right to prospect for minerals upon land falling under the provisions of this act, and also the right to cut without waste and under the general regulations of the forestry board and the supervision of the rangers, timber for the first construction of shanties, prospecting shafts and other necessary structures, from the territories nearest to the prospector's claim or claims. Such license shall be good only for the district in which it is taken out, and shall end at the expiration of one year from the time of its issue, or whenever, sooner than that, the claim is perfected or the prospecting is abandoned. Second, a settler's license shall be granted to any bona fide settler having no timber on his claim, by the local (district) inspector upon the payment of two dollars. Such license shall confer the right, for one year, to cut, for the licensee's own use only and for domestic purposes, timber, fuel and fence material, without waste and under the general regulations of the ferestry board, upon an area of five acres, which the licensee may desigate near his settlement. Third, a timber license shall be granted to any bona fide settler or mine operator or manufacturer, for the purpose of allowing him to supply himself or others with timber, fence material or fuel upon the payment of a license fee of five dollars and the further payment, before beginning to cut any timber, of a sum equal to one dollar for each and every acre embraced in his license, and, in addition, a stumpage of not less than one cent per stump, actual count, before the removal of the timber. Such license shall be granted for one year and shall confer the right to cut the timber on not less than forty nor more than eighty acres, the same to be selected by the applicant and the selection to be approved by the local officer.

Sec. 11. That all licenses provided for in section ten shall be in printed forms, and shall be issued, upon an order from the district inspector, by the receivers of public money upon the payment of the license fee. Licenses shall be numbered in succession, as applications for them are made, and priority of application shall determine the order in which they are granted. The district inspectors shall receive applications for license on certain days of each week, to be published and made known by them. They shall keep open books, in which shall be recorded in proper order applications for license and the action taken upon them, with the names and residence or post office address of the applicants. The inspectors shall also notify the rangers of each license granted in their ranges, and the rangers shall be required to aid licensees in locating their claims. No unused "settler's license" or "timber license" shall be renewed unless good cause is shown for its not having been previously used, nor shall any license be granted to any person who in the use of a previous license has not complied with the regulations of the forestry board. No licenses of any kind shall be transferred from one company to another and continue to be valid unless the transfer of the same is authorized by the forestry board.

LUMBERMEN'S LICENSE.

SEC. 12. That timber on lands of the first-class, which is not needed for mining or agricultural development in the neighborhood, shall be disposed of to lumbermen or others, as it may be applied for under a "lumbermen's license," in quantities not less in amount than that standing or being on one section nor more than that standing or being on twenty-five contiguous sections. Such license shall be granted upon the payment of a fee of twenty-five dollars, by the Commissioner of Forests with the approval of the Secretary of the Interior, under the conditions set forth in section thirteen of this act, and shall confer the right to cut timber and sell the same from as many sections or acres as have been located and paid for. The licensee shall also pay one dollar per acre for the whole number of acres covered by this license, before he may begin operations and not later than six months after the granting of said license. And a further charge of not less than one cent per cubic foot shall be paid by the licensee after the timber has been cut and before the same is renewed. Such license shall be good for two years, and in all cases in which not more than ten sections of timber are embraced in the license it shall not be renewed unless reasons satisfactory to the forestry board are shown why the same could not have been used and its privileges exhausted during the period for which it was first given, nor in any case shall such license be renewed more than once or for a longer term than two years. Where the license embraces more than ten sections of timber the same rule shall apply in regard to its renewal as in the case of licenses for a less amount of timber, except that for every five above ten embraced in the license there may be a renewal of the license for one additional year. No licensee shall be authorized to apply for or take out a second "lumberman's license" until he shall have cut and disposed of three-fourths of the timber to which he is entitled by the license previously given.

SEC. 13. That all applications for "lumberman's license" are to be made to the Commissioner of Forests and must be accompanied by a statement of the location and approximate amount of the timber sought by the applicant, together with a certificate of the local forest inspector to the effect that the lands on which such timber is situated are of the first-class and not covered by any of the local licenses as provided in section ten, nor presumably needed for such within a reasonable time. Such applications shall be considered in the months of August and September only, and no license shall be granted before at least three months have expired from the date of application and the same has been advertised three times in three local papers, if there be so many, of the district in which the licensee intends to locate. If the same location is sought by more than one applicant priority of application shall not rule as to applications made in the same month, but the application for the smallest location shall, in such case, receive first consideration. And wherever a survey of the location is necessary the applicant shall pay half of the expense of such survey, and whenever the licensee begins operations upon his location he must notify the local forest inspector, and all cutting and disposal of the timber and other forest products shall be done under the supervision of the local inspector and in accordance with such regulations as the Commissioner of Forests shall prescribe.

Duties of Forest Commissioner.

Sec. 14. That the Commissioner of Forests shall properly subdivide and arrange into divisions and districts of proper size, such forest lands as shall constitute the forest reserves and forest lands remaining under his control, shall organize a forest service, and appoint inspectors and rangers for the protection and proper administration of said forests, and establish a practicable system of forestry. He shall make reasonable rules and regulations for the prevention of trespass on said lands and for their protection from fire or injury from other causes, and for the conservation of the forest growth, and he shall be empowered, if necessary, on account of any threatened detriment to the forestry interest, and, if the local demand warrants, to have cut and to dispose of any timber which is not taken under the licenses herein provided. The Commissioner of Forests shall have the power to regulate pasturage and any occupancy whatsoever upon the forest lands, and he shall make such other regulations, with the approval of the Secretary of the Interior, as may appear necessary to carry into effect the purposes of this act. He shall make to Congress annually a full and detailed report of his proceedings and those of the assistant commissioners, and all moneys received from the sale of timber or any other privileges he shall pay into the Treasury of the United States.

Co-operation with Other Officers.

Sec. 15. That the Commissioner of the General Land Office, surveyors-general, registers and receivers, and other federal officers connected with the public lands, are directed to co-operate with and assist the Commissioner of Forests to the extent of their power in the selection, classification and management of the public forest lands.

Co-operation with State Boards.

Sec. 16. That whenever any of the States in which public forest lands are situated shall have instituted and provided for a forest commission or other forest management of the forest lands belonging to the State, it shall be in the discretion of the Commissioner of Forests, with the approval of the Secretary of the Interior, to co-operate with such forest commission and to allow the same to act as agents for the United States, under his direction, for the purposes of this act.

Provisions Against Unlawful Cutting.

[To be amended by reference to State laws.]

Sec. 17. That it shall be unlawful to cut, remove, or destroy, or cause or procure to be cut, removed, or destroyed, or aid, counsel, or assist in cutting, removing, or destroying any timber on lands of the United States, except as provided for and permitted by this act, or to wantonly burn, injure, tap, or girdle such timber, or to export, transport, purchase, or dispose of the same, or any lumber, charcoal, pitch, turpentine, or other product manufactured therefrom; and every person violating the provisions of this section shall be guilty of a misdemeanor and shall be liable to a fine of not less than one hundred dollars and not more than one thousand dollars for every such offense, and imprisonment for not more than one year; and every person engaged in such depredation upon timber or timber lands of the United States, whether as principal, agent, employee, carrier, mill owner, manufacturer, vendor or vendee, shall moreover be liable in an action of trespass for the full value of the timber or timber product at the place of delivery; but nothing contained in this section shall prevent any agriculturist or miner from taking from his claim the timber necessary for domestic purposes or the support of his improvements. And whenever there exists a right, previously established by law to cut timber on the public lands, every person or corporation exercising such right must comply with the rules and regulations prescribed by the Commissioner of Forests and approved by the Secretary of the Interior. And all persons acquiring rights to cut timber or any rights of use and occupancy of the forests under the provisions of this act, whether at public sale, by license, or in any other way, are to have and to hold such rights on condition of compliance with the rules and regulations of this act and of the Commissioner of Forests. And a failure to comply with all the rules and regulations so prescribed and approved in regard to the manner of using and occupying the public forest lands shall constitute a misdemeanor punishable as provided in this section.

Occupancy of Forest Lands.

Sec. 18. That it shall be unlawful for any person, firm or corporation knowingly to erect, establish or maintain upon public lands of the United States, without authority from the Commissioner of Forests, any saw-mill or manufactory of lumber or other timber products, or to be engaged or be employed in the manufacture of lumber, charcoal, pitch or turpentine upon public lands, or to use at any such mill, manufactory, or works any timber cut or removed from public lands; and any person violating this section shall be liable to a fine of not less than five hundred and not more than five thousand dollars, in addition to the penalties hereinbefore prescribed; and all mills, manufactories and works so erected and maintained upon public lands shall be absolutely forfeited to the United States.

PENALTIES FOR TRANSPORTING AND HANDLING ILLEGALLY CUT TIMBER.

SEC. 19. That if any master, owner or consignee of any vessel, or any officer or agent of any railroad company, shall knowingly receive for shipment any timber, lumber, or timber product taken without authority from timber lands of the United States, with intent to transport the same to any port or place within the United States, or to export the same to any foreign country, every such master, owner, consignee, officer, agent or railroad company shall be liable to the penalties prescribed in the seventeenth section of this act; and the vessel on board of which any such timber, lumber or timber product shall be taken, transported or seized, shall be wholly forfeited to the United States.

RESTRICTING QUALITY OF FOREST OFFICERS.

SEC. 20. That no person who is directly or indirectly engaged in the manufacture of lumber or timber products, or who is conducting any business which requires a large consumption of timber or wood, shall be qualified to serve as Commissioner of Forests under this act, or to serve in any official capacity in connection with the public forest lands.

REPEALING CLAUSE.

SEC. 21. That the acts of June third, eighteen hundred and seventy-eight, chapters one hundred and fifty and one hundred and fifty-one, and the first and second sections of the act of June fifteenth, eighteen hundred and eighty, entitled "An act relating to the public lands of the United States," and all acts and parts of acts inconsistent with this act, be, and the same are, hereby repealed.

Enacting Clause.

Sec. 22. That this act shall take effect on the first day of July next, but the President may appoint the Commissioner of Forests prior to that date, with his duties and salary to commence at that date.

Appropriation Clause.

Sec. 23. That for the purpose of carrying out the provisions of this act, for the payment of salaries, traveling and other expenses, the sum of five hundred thousand dollars is hereby appropriated.

JOHNS HOPKINS UNIVERSITY

Studies in History and Politics.

Edited by HERBERT B. ADAMS.

Ninth Annual Series 1891.   Price $3.00.

I-II. GOVERNMENT AND ADMINISTRATION OF THE UNITED STATES. By W. W. WILLOUGHBY and W. F. WILLOUGHBY. 75 cents. In boards, interleaved for notes $1.25.

III-IV. UNIVERSITY EDUCATION IN MARYLAND. By B. C. STEINER. THE JOHNS HOPKINS UNIVERSITY (1876-1891). By D. C. GILMAN. With Supplementary Note on University Extension and the University of the Future. By R. G. MOULTON. 50 cents.

V-VI. DEVELOPMENT OF MUNICIPAL UNITY IN THE LOMBARD COMMUNES. By WILLIAM KLAPP WILLIAMS. 50 cents.

VII-VIII. PUBLIC LANDS AND AGRARIAN LAWS OF THE ROMAN REPUBLIC. By ANDREW STEPHENSON. 75 cents.

CONSTITUTIONAL DEVELOPMENT OF JAPAN FROM 1853-1881. By TOYOKICHI IYENAGA.

THE CHARACTER AND INFLUENCE OF THE FUR TRADE IN WISCONSIN. By FREDERICK JACKSON TURNER.

AFRICAN COLONIZATION: A HISTORY OF LIBERIA. By J. H. T. MCPHERSON.

CAUSES OF THE AMERICAN REVOLUTION. By JAMES ALBERT WOODBURN.

UNIVERSITY STUDIES IN SOCIAL SCIENCE. By CHARLES LEE SMITH, JOHN H. FINLEY, A. B. WOODFORD, and others.

HIGHER EDUCATION OF THE PEOPLE. By the EDITOR.

ANNUAL SERIES, 1883-1890.

SERIES I—Local Institutions. 479 pages. $4.00.
SERIES II.—Institutions and Economics. 629 pages. $4.00.
SERIES III.—Maryland, Virginia and Washington. 595 pages. $4.00.
SERIES IV.—Municipal Government and Land Tenure. 600 pages. $3.50.
SERIES V.—Municipal Government, History and Politics. 559 pages. $3.50.
SERIES VI—The History of Co-operation in the United States. 540 pp. $3.50
SERIES VII.—Social Science, Municipal and Federal Government. $3.50.
SERIES VIII.—History, Politics and Education. 625 pp. 8vo. $3.50.

EXTRA VOLUMES.

LOCAL CONSTITUTIONAL HISTORY OF THE UNITED STATES. By GEORGE E. HOWARD, Professor in the University of Nebraska. (*Extra Volumes Four and Five.*)
Vol. I.—Development of the Township, Hundred, and Shire. 526 pages. $3.00.
Vol. II.—Development of the City and the Local Magistracies (in press).

THE NEGRO IN MARYLAND. A Study of the Institution of Slavery. By JEFFREY R. BRACKETT, Ph. D. (*Extra Volume Six*). 270 pages. $2.00.

THE SUPREME COURT OF THE UNITED STATES. By W. W. WILLOUGHBY. 124 pp. 8vo. cloth. $1.25.

THE INTERCOURSE BETWEEN JAPAN AND THE UNITED STATES. INAZO (OTA) NITOBE. 198 pp. 8vo. cloth. $1.25.

STATE AND FEDERAL GOVERNMENT IN SWITZERLAND. By JOHN MARTIN VINCENT. 225 pp. 8vo. cloth. $1.50.

SPANISH INSTITUTIONS IN THE SOUTHWEST. By FRANK W. BLACKMAR. About 300 pp. 8vo. cloth. $2.00.

[This series was begun in 1882. Eight series have been completed, and nine extra volumes issued.

The set of eight series is now offered in a handsome library edition for $24.00, and including subscription to the current (ninth) series, $27.00.

The eight series with nine extra volumes, "New Haven," "Philadelphia," "Baltimore," "Local Constitutional History," Vol. I, "Negro in Maryland," "U. S. Supreme Court," "U. S. and Japan," "Switzerland," and "Spanish Institutions in the Southwest," altogether seventeen volumes, for $38.00.

The nine extra volumes (now ready) will be furnished together for $13.50.

Orders should be addressed to

THE JOHNS HOPKINS PRESS, BALTIMORE, MARYLAND.

Studies in History, Economics and Public Law,

EDITED BY

THE UNIVERSITY FACULTY OF POLITICAL SCIENCE OF COLUMBIA COLLEGE.

The monographs are chosen mainly from among the doctors' dissertions in Political Science, but are not necessarily confined to these. Only those studies are included which form a distinct contribution to science and which are positive works of original research. The monographs are published at irregular intervals, but are paged consecutively as well as separately, so as to form completed volumes.

The first four numbers in the series are:

1. **The Divorce Problem—A Study in Statistics.** By WALTER F. WILLCOX, Ph. D. Price, 50 cents.

2. **The History of Tariff Administrative in the United States, from Colonial Times to the McKinley Administration Bill.** By JOHN DEAN GOSS, Ph. D. Price, 50 cents.

3. **History of Municipal Land Ownership on Manhattan Island.** By GEORGE ASHTON BLACK, Ph. D. (In press.)

4. **Financial History of Massachusetts.** By CHARLES H. J. DOUGLAS. (Ready in October, 1891.)

Other numbers will be announced hereafter.

For further particulars apply to

PROF. EDWIN R. A. SELIGMAN.

Columbia College, New York.

Guggenheimer, Weil & Co.

*A*RE pleased to announce to the readers of this volume their readiness to serve them in any way, from the production of a Visiting Card to a printed volume, of which this is a specimen.

Our Departments:

PRINTING.
- JOB PRINTING.
- BOOK PRINTING.
- CATALOGUE PRINTING.
- LABEL PRINTING.
- RAILROAD PRINTING.

LITHOGRAPHIC.
- SHOW CARDS.
- TOBACCO, CAN-GOODS and other LABELS.
- ADVERTISING CARDS.
- BONDS, CHECKS, Etc.

BOOK BINDING.
- BLANK BOOKS.
- MISCELLANEOUS BINDING.

CARD ENGRAVING.
- WEDDING.
- RECEPTION.
- VISITING.

RETAIL DEPARTMENT:
109 East Baltimore Street.

MECHANICAL DEPARTMENT.
Cor. Lombard and Liberty Sts.

The Quarterly Journal of Economics

PUBLISHED FOR

HARVARD UNIVERSITY

Is established as an aid to investigators and students. It will supply a medium of publication for studies in

Economic History, Criticism, and Speculation,

and for the discussion of the important

Questions of the Day.

It will cordially welcome any real contribution to Economic study, leaving to the writer the sole responsibility for matters of opinion.

The Journal will be issued **October 1; January 1; April 1;** and **July 1.**

It will contain regularly 112 pages 8vo, with such supplementary sheets as may be required from time to time.

Communications for the Editorial management should be addressed to **THE QUARTERLY JOURNAL OF ECONOMICS, Cambridge, Mass.**

Business letters, subscriptions and remittances, to **GEORGE H. ELLIS,** 141 Franklin Street, Boston.

Subscription Price, Two Dollars Per Annum.

Among the writers for numbers already issued were:—

PROF. DUNBAR, of Harvard University.
PROF. FOXWELL, of Cambridge, England.
PROF. HADLEY, of Yale University.
S. DANA HORTON, Esq.
PROF. J. L. LAUGHLIN, Cornell University.
PROF. MARSHALL, of Cambridge, England.
PROF. MACVANE, of Harvard University.
PROF. NASSE, of Bonn, Germany.
PROF. R. M. SMITH, of Columbia College.
PRES. ANDREWS, of Brown University.
A. DE FOVILLE, Paris, France.
PROF. BASTABLE, University of Dublin.
PROF. GIDDINGS, Bryn Mawr College.
F. J. STIMSON, Esq.
PROF. TAUSSIG, of Harvard University.
PRES. WALKER, of the Mass. Institute of Technology.
CARROLL D. WRIGHT, of the National Labor Bureau.
JAMES BONAR, London, England.
STUART WOOD, Philadelphia, Pa.
PROF. PATTEN, University of Pennsylvania.
SEYMOUR DEXTER, Esq.
N. P. GILMAN, Esq.
PROF. BOEHM-BAWERK, Vienna, Austria

CONTENTS FOR JULY, 1890.

I.—CO-OPERATIVE PRODUCTION IN FRANCE AND ENGLAND. EDWARD CUMMINGS.
II.—THE RESIDUAL THEORY OF DISTRIBUTION. FREDERICK B. HAWLEY.
III.—THE SILVER SITUATION. HORACE WHITE.
IV.—FREDERICK LE PLAY. H. HIGGS.
NOTES AND MEMORANDA.
    The Conversion of the English Debt. A. C. MILLER.
    Changes in the Form of Railroad Capital. THOMAS L. GREEN.
RECENT PUBLICATIONS UPON ECONOMICS.

APPENDIX.
A FAMILY MONOGRAPH OF LE PLAY'S.
THE RAMPAL LEGACY TO AID CO-OPERATIVE SOCIETIES.

CONTENTS FOR OCTOBER, 1890.

I.—SOME EXPERIMENTS ON BEHALF OF THE UNEMPLOYED. AMOS G. WARNER.
II.—BOEHM-BAWERK ON VALUE AND WAGES. S. M. MACVANE.
III.—A CENTURY OF PATENT LAW. CHAUNCEY SMITH.
IV.—THE SOUTHERN RAILWAY AND STEAMSHIP ASSOCIATION. HENRY HUDSON.
NOTES AND MEMORANDA.
    Studies on the Origin of the French Economists. STEPHEN BAUER.
RECENT PUBLICATIONS UPON ECONOMICS.

APPENDIX.
STATISTICS ON THE GERMAN LABORERS' COLONIES.
AGREEMENT OF THE SOUTHERN RAILWAY AND STEAMSHIP ASSOCIATION.

PUBLICATIONS OF THE UNIVERSITY OF PENNSYLVANIA.

Political Economy and Public Law Series.

EDMUND J. JAMES, Ph. D., Editor.

This series consists of a number of valuable monographs representing the fruit of the most recent research upon the subjects of which they treat. Up to the present time, two volumes have appeared.

VOLUME I
Consisting of the following eight numbers:

No. 1.—Wharton School Annals of Political Science. (Out of print.)
No. 2.—Anti-Rent Agitation. Prof. E. P. Cheyney. Price, 50 cents.
No. 3.—Ground Rents in Philadelphia. Boies Penrose, of the Philadelphia Bar. Price, 25 cents.
No. 4.—Consumption of Wealth. Prof. S. N. Patten. Price, 50 cents.
No. 5.—Prison Statistics. Dr. Roland P. Falkner. Price, 25 cents.
No. 6.—Rational Principles of Taxation. Prof. S. N. Patten. Price, 50 cents.
No. 7.—Federal Constitution of Germany, with Historical Introduction. Prof. E. J. James. Price, 50 cents.
No. 8.—Federal Constitution of Switzerland. Translated by Prof. E. J. James. Price, 50 cents.
Price of Nos. 2 to 8 in one order $2.40.

VOLUME II.

Our Sheep and the Tariff. William Draper Lewis, Ph.D., late Fellow in Wharton School of Finance and Economy. Price, cloth, $2.00.

VOLUME III.

The first two numbers of the third volume are announced for early publication.

No. 1.—The Federal Council of Germany. A study in comparative constitutional law. Prof. James Harvey Robinson.
This institution is the very centre and core of the existing form of government in Germany, and deserves to be much better known by students of constitutional government.

No. 2.—The Theory of Dynamic Economics. Prof. Simon N. Patten.
A review and criticism of the new political economy from the standpoint of consumption.

PUBLICATIONS OF THE UNIVERSITY OF PENNSYLVANIA.

Wharton School Studies in Politics and Economics.

This series will consist of monographs by the students of the Wharton School of Finance and Economy.

NUMBER I
Which has just appeared is entitled:

The Recent Development of American Industries. By The Class of 91. Price, 50 cents; cloth, $1.00.

PUBLICATIONS
OF THE
American Academy of Political and Social Science
Sent free to all members of the Academy in the form of
THE ANNALS.
SUBSCRIPTION PRICE TO OTHERS THAN MEMBERS, $6.00 PER YEAR.

SPECIAL RATE TO LIBRARIES, $5.00.

SEPARATE EDITIONS.
Price of each number, unless otherwise indicated, 50 cents.
Nos. 1-26 in one order, $7.00.

1890.
1. *Canada and the United States.* J. G. Bourinot.
2. *Decay of Local Government in America.* Simon N. Patten.
3. *Law of Wages and Interest.* J. B. Clark.
4. *Province of Sociology.* F. H. Giddings.
5. *Instruction in Public Law and Economics in Germany.* Leo H. Rowe.
6. *Railroad Passenger Fares in Hungary.* Jane J. Wetherell.
7. *The Origin of Connecticut Towns.* Charles M. Andrews.
8. *The Original Package Case.* C. Stuart Patterson.
9. *Original Features in the United States Constitution.* James Harvey Robinson.
10. *Historical vs. Deductive Political Economy.* E. v. Boehm-Bawerk.
11. *Instruction in Public Law and Economics in Germany.* II.

1891.
12. *The Austrian Economists.* E. v. Boehm-Bawerk.
13. *On the Conception of Sovereignty.* David G. Ritchie.
14. *The Character of Villein Tenure.* W. J. Ashley.
15. *A Critique of Wages Theories.* Stuart Wood.
16. *Railroad Passenger Tariffs in Austria.* Jane J. Wetherell.
17. *Public Health and Municipal Government.* Dr. J. S. Billings.
18. *History of Statistics.* Meitzen-Falkner. $1.25.
19. *The Genesis of a Written Constitution.* William C. Morey.
20. *Natural Law.* Fred M. Taylor.
21. *On the Concept of Wealth.* C. A. Tuttle.
22. *Compulsory Voting.* F. W. Hollis.
23. *Instruction in Economics in Italy.* Roland P. Falkner.
24. *The Philadelphia Social Science Association.* Joseph G. Rosengarten.
25. *Theorie and Technique of Statistics.* Meitzen-Falkner. $1.50.
26. *Handbook of the Academy—List of Members, etc.* $2.00.
27. *Constitution of Mexico.* Bernard Moses.
28. *Land Transfer Reform.* J. W. Jenks.
29. *Economic Basis of Prohibition.* Simon N. Patten.
30. *International Liability for Mob Injuries.* E. W. Huffcutt.
31. *Political Science at Oxford.* D. G. Ritchie.

Numbers 1 to 31 in one order $8.00.

The above numbers which together with Proceedings of the Academy, Personal Notes, Book Notes and Miscellany, constitute the publications of the American Academy of Political and Social Science, were also issued in the ANNALS WITH SUPPLEMENTS, in which form they were sent FREE to all members of the Academy.

Annual membership fee $5.00.

Subscriptions for the publications and applications for membership should be addressed

AMERICAN ACADEMY OF POLITICAL AND SOCIAL SCIENCE,
Station B, Philadelphia, Pa.

Papers of the American Historical Association.

Four volumes of the Proceedings of the American Historical Association, indexed and handsomely bound in dark blue cloth, with gilt top, have been published by G. P. Putnam's Son's, 27 and 29 West 23rd street, New York City. These volumes will be sent post paid, at $5 each, to subscribers.

Members of the Association, on payment of 75 cents to the publishers, will receive post paid any one of these bound volumes in exchange for unbound numbers with title page and index, if returned prepaid in good condition for binding.

VOLUME I. contains the report of the organization and proceedings of the Association at Saratoga in 1884, and also the proceedings for 1885, with special papers by Andrew D. White, on "Studies in General History and the History of Civilization;" by Dr. George W. Knight, on "The History and Management of Federal Land Grants for Education in the Northwest Territory;" "The Louisiana Purchase in its Influence upon the American System," by Rt. Rev. C. F. Robertson, Bishop of Missouri; and a "History of the Appointing Power of the President," by Professor Lucy M. Salmon, of Vassar College.

VOLUME II. contains the report of the proceedings in Washington in 1886, with special papers on "The History of the Doctrine of Comets," by Andrew D. White; "Willem Usselinx, Founder of the Dutch and Swedish West India Companies," by Dr. J. F. Jameson; "Church and State in the United States," by Dr. Philip Schaff.

VOLUME III. contains reports of the proceedings in Boston and Cambridge in 1887 and in Washington in 1888. Most of the papers read at these two conventions are here printed in full.

VOLUME IV. contains a report of the proceedings at the Washington meeting in 1889. With this volume began the system of publication in quarterly parts, embracing groups of papers and important single monographs like that of Dr. G. Brown Goode, on "The Origin of the National Scientific and Educational Institutions of the United States."

VOLUME V. is now in progress. Parts 2 and 3 were issued together. Part 3, the July number, is now ready.

Since the incorporation of the American Historical Association by Congress in 1889, the society has been associated with the Smithsonian Institution and through Secretary Langley reports annually to Congress. The report for the year 1889 contains a general account of the proceedings in Washington that year, the inaugural address of President C. K. Adams, a paper on "The Spirit of Historical Research," by James Schouler, and a reprint of Dr. Goode's paper on "The Origin of the National Scientific and Educational Institutions of the United States," together with Mr. P. L. Ford's Bibliography of the published works of members of the American Historical Association. The report for 1890 will contain an account of the proceedings in Washington for that year, abstracts of all the papers read, John Jay's inaugural address on "The Demand for Education in American History," a supplementary bibliography of the published works of members, and the first part of a bibliography of the publications of State Historical Societies in this country. These reports are issued free to members of the Association, and can be obtained by others through Members of Congress.

Address all orders for the regular series to G. P. Putnam's Sons, 27 and 29 West 23d St., New York City.

www.ingramcontent.com/pod-product-compliance
Lightning Source LLC
Chambersburg PA
CBHW020143170426
43199CB00010B/867